D0945176

What others are saying about

Building Better Humans:

"*Wonderful! Good solid parenting advice, presented in a voice to which parents will easily relate. I love that the entire approach to parenting rests on sensible principles and guiding philosophies of parenting that are well grounded in common sense. The authors' experience as parents is obvious, not only in the content of the book but also in how 'real' they are; the examples are ones to which all of us, professionals and parents alike, can relate. I laughed at times, sighed at times, and relived some of my own triumphs and mistakes in my dual roles as parent and child psychologist. And that candidness as authors makes for a very approachable, comfortable book whose wisdom is surrounded by humor and humility.*"

Dr. Sandra Siegel, Ph.D., Child Clinical Psychologist

"*I nodded in agreement at the parenting wisdom in this book, and laughed heartily in identification with many of the scenarios presented in* Building Better Humans. *If you're looking for some down-to-earth answers to everyday parenting challenges, you will not be disappointed by* Building Better Humans."

Christine Field, Author, Attorney, Speaker, www.realmomlife.com

"For most parents, the art of parenting is far from simple. While often a joy, parenting can also be challenging, frustrating, and stressful! That said, David and Lisa Davoust are to the rescue. Their book, Building Better Humans, *is the most practical and well written book I have ever read on the subject. Their advice is psychologically sound, easy to implement, and comes from a solid set of values. If you follow their guidelines and suggestions, your children are sure to benefit from it and you might even save yourself some stress in the process. I give this book my highest recommendation."*

Tim Ursiny, Ph.D., RCC, CBC, Author of
The Coward's Guide to Conflict and *The Top Performer's Guide to Attitude*

"Practical is a key descriptor for this helpful guide to parenting. For the parent who needs some 'down-to-earth' guidelines based on sound principles, this book can give hope and motivation. Specific examples were both sensible and doable.

"I found it to be very well written, readable, clear, to the point, and engaging. The Davousts had a knack for anticipating my questions as I went along and dealing with them before the end of the chapter.

"I especially resonated with the chapter on 'Kids in Crisis.' They did a superb job of covering the major problem areas and practical helps during these troubling heart wrenching, times. That chapter alone should be useful for the parents who may be inclined to say, 'They make parenting sound so easy, they don't have MY kids.'"

Chuck Lewis, Ph.D, Counselor, Barnabas International,
Retired Director of Counseling, Wheaton College

Building Better Humans

Building Better Humans

By David & Lisa Davoust

With illustrations by Abigail Davoust

BUILDING BETTER HUMANS

Published by Robis Publishing

P.O Box 39, Wheaton, IL 60187

Printed in the United States of America

First Edition 2014

ISBN 978-0-9707573-1-9 (PAPERBACK)

ISBN 978-0-9707573-2-6 (ELECTRONIC BOOK TEXT)

ISBN 978-0-9707573-3-3 (HARDBACK)

ISBN 978-0-9707573-4-0 (DOWNLOADABLE AUDIO FILE)

DEDICATED TO:
Rob, Caroline, and Michael

| Table of Contents |

| Introduction |

Parenthood can feel overwhelming at times. Kids will fight for what they want, and often they win by simply wearing their parents down. This can be true with just one child, but it becomes much more difficult when the kids outnumber the adults. Whether you're just starting out with your first baby or are in the middle of the difficult teenage years, this book is designed to give you immediate help. We hope it will help you learn techniques to take charge of your family and create an environment to help your children grow into healthy, productive adults.

In these pages we will present twelve basic parenting principles. If you learn and apply these simple principles, your house will become happier and more peaceful. We say simple principles because they are simple to learn and understand, and you can apply them immediately. Parenting is not complicated. It is not like learning the piano; such a skill is difficult, and you can spend a lifetime trying to master it and still not be great at it.

Parenting, on the other hand, is more like running a marathon. You can learn the principles of long-distance running in a matter of minutes. However, to actually complete a marathon takes patience, diligence, and many hours of work. During all those times of running, you have to keep your mind's eye on the finish line, or you will give up and go back to everyday living. (We've gone so far as to register for a half marathon, but have not followed up on that commitment with the necessary physical preparation!) Like running, parenting is not complicated, but it can be difficult and sometimes tedious. Above all, kids need consistent, calm, sane parents—the very thing they seem to be constantly fighting against.

Are you ready to make a big difference in your family with some simple principles? Let's get started.

A Word about Voice

In *Building Better Humans,* we have sought to share the principles we have learned from raising our own children and from our experience teaching on marriage and family. Because many of our stories are very personal, we have found it easier to have just one of us narrate the story. That task has fallen to me, David. So throughout the book, there will be times when I refer to myself as "I" even though the book is co-authored by Lisa. It is our hope that this will not be distracting and instead will provide you, the reader, with a richer understanding of our personal successes and failures in applying these simple principles of parenting.

| Your Role as the Parent |

"Train up a child in the way he should go,
and when he is old, he will not depart from it."

A PROVERB OF SOLOMON

Understanding your job as a parent is the first key to success. If you were hired to work at a new company and didn't know what your job was, how long do you think you would last? It is interesting that parenting is such a vital part of our society and yet most of us, as parents, are just kind of making it up as we go. We have no clear job description and are not even quite sure what we are trying to accomplish.

So what is our role? We often hear parents say, "I just want my children to be happy." This sounds like a good goal on the surface, but if this is truly your guiding principle, it will lead you to make bad choices for your kids. If you are doing your job as a parent, there are times when you are definitely going to make them unhappy. We instinctively know this when they are babies. When our first son was just a few days old, we had to take him to the doctor for a medical procedure. We still remember his little baby scream of pain. As his parents, it was one of the worst sounds we had ever heard. We hated it. We never wanted to hear that sound again. But we knew that this brief pain was necessary for him to lead a healthy life. If we had to do it all over again, we would do exactly the same thing (although maybe next time we would wait where we couldn't hear his scream).

As our children grow, there are many times when we have to make them temporarily unhappy for their longer-term good. Why do we not let them eat candy all day long? Because we know that so much sugar is not good for them. Why do we keep them from running headlong into the street after a ball? Because we know that the happiness of the moment would quickly end with an oncoming car. Our younger son liked to jump into swimming pools, even when he was a toddler. He had no fear. We often had to make him unhappy by keeping him away from swimming pools so he wouldn't drown.

A swimming pool is actually a good analogy for parenting. If you think of the local public swimming pool, there are many jobs required to service the kids.

There is the CASHIER or GATEKEEPER who only lets authorized people into the pool area and who handles the money.

There is the FOOD VENDOR who offers things like ice cream, hamburgers, and hot dogs.

There is the LIFEGUARD who keeps the kids from drowning and sometimes seems like he is spoiling all the fun.

There is the FIRST AID person who is there to patch up the skinned knees and bloody noses of those kids who ignore the lifeguard.

There is the swim COACH who teaches the kids how to swim using the ever-irritating whistle and a yell that can be heard underwater.

And there is even the pool CLEANER who cleans all the leaves and other nasty stuff out of the pool, straightens up the chairs, cleans up the spilled ice cream, and empties the garbage cans.

As a parent, you do all of these jobs for your kids.

You are the CASHIER/GATEKEEPER who takes care of the money and who makes sure not to let dangerous people into your kids' lives.

You are the FOOD VENDOR who gets to provide them with ice cream and hot dogs and all the other food that keeps them going.

You are the LIFE GUARD who jumps in to save them when they are in over their heads.

You are the one who gives them FIRST AID when they get hurt.

You are the COACH who teaches them how to swim so they don't drown.

And you are even the one who CLEANS up after them when they have had too much sun and ice cream.

All of these roles are part of running a pool and part of running a family. But just as one person could not successfully do all of these jobs at a swimming pool without help, if you are trying to give equal focus to every parenting task, you will be constantly frustrated. No wonder we often feel so guilty as parents. The task is really overwhelming, and there is always something else we can think of that the "good" parent would be doing, like making their children's lunches every day or building a go-kart together.

It sounds kind of silly to me now, but I used to feel like a failure as a parent because I never built a go-kart with our oldest son. He and I always talked about it, but we never got around to it. We parents have this movie image of the perfect parent playing ball in the front yard with the kids every night, and when reality doesn't quite match that, or worse, when the kids don't even *want* to play ball with us, we can feel like a failure.

But we have good news for you. Being a good parent does not mean doing all of your parental tasks equally well. In fact, if we understand what our primary job is, not only will we be better parents, but we will lead less frantic, busy, guilt-ridden lives.

The truth is that just as in any other job, parents do have *one* primary responsibility. When we understand what that is, it helps us to make better choices and prioritize our activities. What is that primary role? If we think of the swimming pool analogy again, it is hard to imagine what jobs we could stop doing. We have to protect the kids from drowning each other, right? We have to keep the pool clean, right? We have to keep the kids fed, right? What could we possibly stop doing?

The key is to change our perspective. It's easy to focus on how to benefit the kids right now while they are swimming in our guarded pool. But we have to remember that all too soon, they will be out in the world swimming in the unguarded river of life. All our efforts to watch over them and clean up after them and feed them will have little benefit when they are away from us.

So it turns out that our primary job is to make sure they can survive when they are away from us. In our analogy, this would be the SWIM COACH. Why is this the most important role? Because our primary job is to prepare our kids to be able to swim in the real world where there isn't a lifeguard to jump in and save them. **Our goal should be to raise up children who can be positive members of society when we are not around to take care of them.**

Did you ever take swim lessons? Did the coach make you happy? If they were good, they could often make the lessons fun, but most of the time they just focused on making you do the work. Why? Because they knew they only had you for a limited amount of time, and they had their eyes constantly on the main task of teaching you how to swim.

If we don't keep the end goal in mind, we can end up spending all of our time just keeping the pool clean, and we won't have time to teach the kids to swim, which means that they are not going to be ready when they are thrown into the deep end of life.

Some parents realize that swimming is dangerous business, so they spend all their time trying to keep their children safe. They have taken on the role of lifeguard. "Don't run. Don't horseplay. Stay off the rocks." Lifeguards are important. They are the ones that dive in to save the child when he is drowning. The problem with the "lifeguard parent" is that they are not preparing the child for the future. The child is kept safe at home, but as soon as they are away from the parent, they are subject to risks for which they are unprepared. Those risks might be at school or in the neighborhood, or maybe, if you are a really good lifeguard, those risks won't appear until they move away from home. But those risks will come, and if you have always protected your children, they will be largely unprepared for life and, consequently, may spend much of their lives feeling like they are drowning.

Remember our youngest son who liked to jump into swimming pools? We had to teach him how to swim early because we never knew when he might jump into a swimming pool at a time when

BBH Principle #1

Your primary role as a parent is to prepare your children for life without you.

our backs were turned. Once he learned to swim, we had less to worry about and he had a new source of enjoyment. As parents, our primary job is to teach our children the skills they need so they can survive in the waters of life when we are not around. That means we have to teach them how to swim, how to handle rough water, and how to help other swimmers.

What are you supposed to teach them?

What do we mean when we say our main job is to teach our children to swim? It may be difficult for some parents to accept, but **our primary role is to prepare our kids for life without us.** That means we need to teach them principles to live by in every area of life: cooking, cleaning, interacting with others, school, work, love, marriage, sex, entertainment … no lesson is off-limits!

But here is the key, and we will talk about this more in chapter 3: you can't just teach your kids rules, because rules won't stand up to the "whys" from their friends or their spouse or even their own conscience. You need to teach them the principles to live by—the reasons behind the rules.

There is an old story about a young woman who got married. Whenever she made a pot roast, she cut off both ends of the roast before cooking it. Her husband kept asking her, "Why do you do that? You are wasting that meat." But she just answered, "That's the way it is done." Finally, tired of having this argument with her husband, she asked her mom, "Why do we cut off both ends of the roast before cooking it?" To which her mother replied, "Well, I just did it because that is the only way it would fit into my pan." The young wife had learned the steps, but not the principle—and had wasted a lot of meat along the way.

In most cases, the principles are *more important* than the rules. If we can go back to our swimming pool analogy, one thing that lifeguards are taught is not to directly approach a drowning person. If they are only taught this rule and not the reason behind it, they are likely to forget it in the heat of helping someone. But the why is very important. You should not directly approach a person who is drowning, because the victim is not in his right mind. He will climb on top of his would-be rescuer to keep from drowning, and in the process risk drowning them both. So lifeguards are taught to first use other lifesaving methods such as a pole or life ring, and if that doesn't work, to approach the swimmer from behind, where they can safely drag him towards shore without endangering themselves. The principle is important to understand in order for the lifeguard to apply the rule properly.

Your goal is to teach principles that your kids can then apply to situations they face even when you are not there to advise them. For example, you might have a rule that says, "No R-rated movies," which is fine to start. But what is the principle you are teaching the kids? It is better to teach them *why* you have that rule. In our house, when the kids wanted to watch something we didn't approve of, we asked them, "How will watching that make you a better person or add anything positive to your life?" We taught them the principle of considering what they were feeding their minds and their hearts. If their friends wanted to watch a horror movie, for example, we would ask, "Do you want those images in your mind? You will never be able to erase them." Of course, this means the kids can challenge our watching habits on those same principles, but that is a good thing too. We will discuss rules and principles in greater depth in chapter 3.

The Freedom of Your Primary Role

Understanding your role should actually be freeing for you, because it helps you realize that your primary purpose is not to clean up after your kids, but instead to teach them how to clean up after themselves. It is not to serve them, but to teach them to serve one another. It is not to cook for them, but to teach them how to cook for themselves—you get the idea. Your job is to prepare them to live without you.

As parents, we want to do nice things for our kids, but sometimes those very acts of kindness can be a disservice to their development. For example, some moms continue to do their children's laundry well into adulthood. We know one young man who has never done a load of laundry in his life. When he was in college, he would simply Febreze his dirty clothes all semester long and then bring them home for Mom to wash during breaks. Mom was showing great love, but in the process, her son was not well prepared for life or eventual marriage, and now that he's married he may have some unnecessary disagreements with his new wife.

Why not start teaching your kids how to do their laundry as soon as they are old enough to operate the washing machine? Sure, they might occasionally end up with pink underwear, but that is all part of learning. (As long as they are just doing their own clothes and not yours!) Having them do their own laundry not only teaches them a particular skill, it also trains them to take care of their own stuff and helps teach the larger lesson of personal responsibility.

You can teach your kids to clean at almost any age. You just need to make the lessons age-appropriate. If a 4-year-old picks up her toys but puts them in the wrong place, praise her effort. Resist the urge to fix it. If your 8-year-old cleans off the table but misses some specks of food, don't go back and re-clean it. Otherwise you may send a message to him that his efforts don't matter. Of course, by the time he is 14, you should probably make him do it over again until it is right—but that is teaching a different lesson. What you expect from your kids should be age-appropriate, but you should expect something from them. Everyone rises to the expectations of others— especially their parents. If you expect nothing from your kids, that is exactly what you will get. As soon as our kids were old enough, we made them take turns doing the dishes. Giving kids regular house-hold chores helps teach them that a well-formed person pitches in and helps the group. Where better to start that lesson than at home in the family?

Another suggestion is to teach your children that there are differ-ent levels of clean for different occasions. For example, if you require your children to clean their bedrooms on a regular basis, the task probably doesn't always need to be completed to the same level of perfection as if you have a visitor coming who will be staying in their room. If you try to make your kids always be perfect, they are more likely to rebel and may even develop some neurotic tendencies as well. In the real world, most of us don't have time to do every chore perfectly every time. Instead, we do some chores "good enough" depending on the situation. Being real with our kids means teach-ing them that there are acceptable levels of effort depending on the circumstances. In our house we have "regular clean" and "Mommy clean." If we ask the kids to clean the kitchen on a normal day, they will do most of the dishes and maybe wipe down the counters. But if we tell them we want it "Mommy clean," they know that we want it to look like it does when Mom cleans. That means *all* the dishes are washed, including the pots and pans; it means cleaning all the counters and wiping down the stove; it might even mean sweeping the floor.

· What are other skills that you want your child to know when they are launched out in life? Teach them now. Don't always fix their broken things, teach them how to fix them. Even if you are not a handy person yourself and don't do repairs around your house, you can show your kids how you select the person to do the work, what the considerations are, etc. Teach them how to handle a similar situation when they are out on their own. Does your child need help with homework? Don't finish it for her. Instead, help her by talking her through it and teaching her methods for solving problems that will apply beyond this assignment. We have had a lot of fun helping our teenage children with their school papers, not by writing them for them, but by discussing their approach, encouraging their creativity, and showing them how to research effectively. Not only has this taught them how to write a better paper, but it has given us the opportunity to call out and encourage strengths in our kids that we wouldn't otherwise have noticed.

Helping your kids to accomplish something can be much more rewarding than just doing it for them. When our youngest son was 12, he saw an ad for a T-shirt that he was sure his older sister would like. She is kind of short, and the shirt was from the Dr. Seuss story *Horton Hears a Who*. It said, "A Person's a Person No Matter How Small." We thought this was nice of him, so we drove him to the store to purchase the shirt. Unfortunately, they were out of stock and the shirt design had been discontinued. He was very disappointed, so we showed him how he could look up other locations of that store on the Internet and call them to see if they had that shirt. He came to our office and began calling stores, first locally and then all over the country, to try to find that shirt. After several hours of calls, we were so worried that all of his effort would lead to disappointment. But he did not give up. He came back and made more calls the next day, and he finally found one T-shirt on the East Coast. We helped him order it and have it shipped. The process taught him how to converse with people on the phone, showed him the value of persistence, and helped to strengthen the love between him and his sister. His sister was very impressed not just with the shirt, but with the amount of personal effort that went into finding it.

As parents, we like to be able to help our kids. We want to jump in and save them. It makes us feel good. It validates us as parents. And there are times when you will have to jump in and save them— like our toddler with the swimming pool. But there are times when parents get so much satisfaction from helping their child that they subconsciously don't *want* the child to learn how to do it. This can often be the case when a mom keeps doing the laundry for her grown child. Mom feels useful doing her son's laundry, so she doesn't really want him to do it. But parenting isn't about what makes us feel good; it is about what is best for our child.

Right now, your daughter is playing in a nice, safe, guarded pool, but someday she is going to be thrown into the rushing river of life, and it is not your job to save her from life, but to prepare her for it. Ask yourself, "What do I wish I had known how to do when I started out in life?" Teach your kids those things.

Of course, the things we teach our children should go way beyond just how to take care of themselves. Think of the character traits you want to teach them: compassion, generosity, love, faithfulness, truthfulness, patience. These are all examples of traits we can form in our children if we work on them proactively. More on those later.

The bottom line is that for us to be effective in our job as a parent, we need to always keep in mind what our primary role is. It isn't to make our kids happy; it is to prepare them for life in the real world. Remember that they will eventually make their own choices. We should want them to start making those choices while we are still around to help direct them. Our job is to give them the tools to make good choices and prepare them for a life independent of us. They have the best chance of being healthy and joyful if we have passed on the right principles.

NEXT STEPS:

- Consider what you want your children to be like when they are all grown up.

- What practical life skills will they need?

- What character traits would you like to see in them?

- How do you want them to treat others?

- Discuss your answers to these questions with the other parent so you are in agreement.

- Don't be afraid to tell your children what your role is and what your goals are for them. Having everyone understand their respective roles can actually make your relationship less stressful.

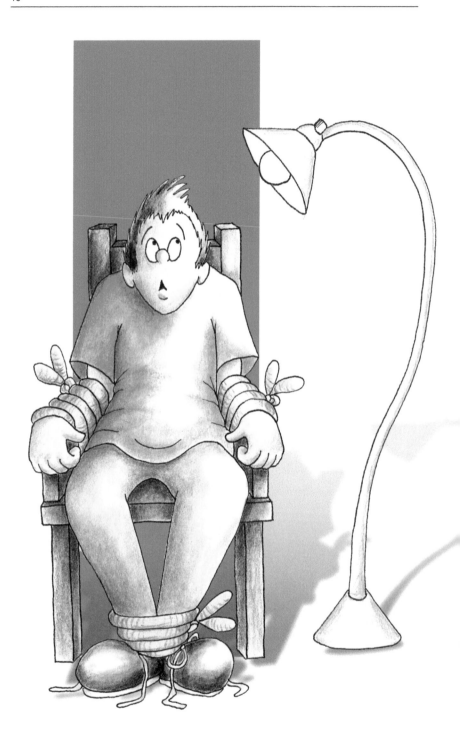

| Getting Your Child to Communicate |

*"If someone forces you to go one mile,
go with him two miles."*

THE SERMON ON THE MOUNT

*"Tune your ear to wisdom and apply
your heart to understanding."*

A PROVERB OF SOLOMON

M any parents complain that their teenage children don't talk to them. But if you think back to when your children were really young, you probably didn't have that problem. In fact, most parents of toddlers will tell you that the problem is that their kids won't *stop* talking. They talk constantly about everything and nothing, and it can be really wearing on parental sanity to hear for the hundredth time about how Squirtle becomes Blastoise. But then somewhere along the way kids just stop communicating with their parents. The truth is that *not* talking to you is a learned response.

When I was growing up, my dad would look up from his newspaper and ask me, "So, how are things at school?" I would give him a detailed answer about how things were going while he continued to read his newspaper. After a little while, he would look up again and say, "So, how are things at school?" I quickly learned that he was not truly interested in the answer—and that led me to believe that he was not truly interested in me. So my answers changed from a detailed description of the woes of childhood angst to the pat answer of, "Fine."

Of course, you don't have to be as blatant as my dad. Kids quickly pick up on our pained looks when they delve into an explanation of their latest video game or into a story of why Barbie and Ken are fighting today.

When kids think we don't value what they have to say, or worse, if they think every conversation is just a chance for us to judge their opinions, they are going to quickly find someone else to talk to. You might think your child doesn't talk, but you may be surprised to discover the depth of conversation they have with their friends.

The problem is that parents often only want to talk about what is "important": things like school, grades, relationships, friends, sex, drugs, etc., and they don't want to waste time on the frivolous stuff. Unfortunately, the important stuff is often surrounded by what we consider unimportant.

So how can you get your kids to talk to you? The answer is simple. If you want your child to talk to you about the stuff you consider important, you have to listen to what is important to them first.

This principle is most effectively applied if you start when your child is very young, but you can begin at any age. The key is to be interested in the things that interest them. Things like Barbies, American Girl Dolls, Pokémon, cartoons, and video games—all those things that as an adult you might consider to be of little value. If you communicate to your kids that the things that are important to them have no value, what they hear is that *they* have no value. You want your kids to talk to you? Get them talking to you about what they enjoy now, and when they get older they will talk to you about *everything*.

BBH Principle #2

If you want your child to talk to you about the stuff you consider important, you have to listen to what is important to them first.

You cannot just pretend to listen. Try to approach each conversation with the expectation that they will have something valuable to say. Are you wondering what you will begin to talk about? You have to actually get involved in what they are involved in. When our children were young, they were into Pokémon trading cards and video games. So in order to get into their world, we collected Pokémon cards with them and played the game. We spent a lot of money and time seeking the rarest Pokémon cards. We had many conversations with the kids about the relative worth of Pidgeot and Squirtle, and we felt like we lost a few years of our lives sitting through the Pokémon movie. However, that time invested helped create the foundation of relationship that allowed us to talk to our children about anything.

Of course, for teenage children, their interests aren't going to be Pokémon or Barbies, they will be music, movies, YouTube videos, and things like that. Is your child into a band? Get to know that band. Find *something* about them that you can appreciate. Talk about the songs. Buy some of your own. Go to a concert. Build a memory with your child over that interest. Show interest where their interest is. Our youngest son is a chess player, so I started playing chess. I developed it as an interest by playing online, not just when I was with him. He is a lot better than I am, but it gives us another connection point—and it is fun, too.

Building Memories

Another touch point that will help you build a strong relationship with your child is building memories together. There is no substitute for time spent together. Trips to special places and special events are very important, such as family vacations. But you also have to be intentional to build individual shared memories with each child. Each of us wants to feel special, and each child needs something that is just theirs. When our daughter was in junior high, she and I began attending a yearly event called Night of Joy, which is held at Disney World each fall. I took her out of school for two days, and she and I spent a long weekend listening to a variety of music groups that she liked and just generally hanging out together. During this time we did a lot of talking. We talked about the bands, we talked about the family, we talked about school. Sometimes we talked about nothing at all, but we built a relationship that made it easy for her to talk to us about anything.

For one of our sons who was interested in cooking, we made it a tradition to go to a food festival together. For our oldest son, we did a weeklong canoeing trip through the boundary waters—just dad and son. There is no substitute for time spent together.

But your memory-building does not always need to be extravagant; it just needs to be something focused on that child. We make it a habit for each of us (Mom and Dad) to get regular one-on-one time with each child even if that is just going out to dinner together. For my dad, it meant joining the Indian Guides and participating in

Indian Guide activities. I am pretty sure my 40-year-old dad did not want to spend time making tomahawks and things like that, but he went with me, and that strengthened our relationship—it gave us a much-needed connection point.

Another way you can build memories and develop your relationship is to celebrate together. Things like graduations and birthdays are obvious times to celebrate, but you can also celebrate smaller accomplishments along the way. In our family, birthdays are a *really* big deal. Our celebration shows each person that they are important. On their birthday, each person is the "birthday boss." They get to preempt one of the parents from the front seat of the car, pick dinner, and choose what we do with our free time. And they don't have to do any chores that day. One of the best birthday traditions Lisa started is "appreciation time." At some point during the birthday dinner, we go around the table and each family member says one thing they appreciate about the birthday person. These times have been a huge blessing in our family. The birthday person gets to hear some great encouragement even from their brothers and sisters, and everyone gets practice at speaking kind words. These are some of the best shared memories, and the activity even draws the kids closer to each other.

You can even create opportunities to build memories. In our family, we celebrate Walt Disney's birthday with a birthday cake. Lisa's parents celebrated Mozart's birthday. What family couldn't use a little more partying together? (And cake!) Be creative!

An Atmosphere of Communication

Another way you can get your kids to communicate with you is to create an atmosphere of open communication.

My dad was an over-stressed business owner who could be kind of hot-tempered and was not the easiest person to talk to. However, he did one thing in terms of communication that we thought was pretty cool. He had a policy called *Free Time.* Any kid in the family could ask him for *Free Time.* If he granted it, then for that period of time, we could tell him anything or ask him anything, and he was not allowed to get mad. So if we really wanted to know something, or if we just wrecked the car and wanted to tell him about it without him overreacting, we could ask for *Free Time.* The interesting thing is that we six kids held this *Free Time* as something almost sacred, and thus we rarely used it. But it was great to know it was there.

Lisa and I do something a little different. We sort of have a constant *Free Time* going. Lisa set the tone for this early in our married life, and we credit this approach for much of the great communication we have had with our kids. From as early as they could understand, we made it clear to our kids that they can ask us anything. And we mean *anything!* No subject is off-limits: God, sex, drugs, drinking, homosexuality, war, Osama Bin Laden ... anything. Of course, the answers we give to their questions are age-appropriate, but we make sure to always give honest answers. There were no cabbage patch stories of where kids come from, but when a 4-year-old asks where babies come from, they don't need a detailed reproductive lesson either; they can get an abbreviated understanding that babies come from Mommies and Daddies. Children need just enough information to satisfy their current question, and they can come back with follow-up questions if they want to know more.

Don't ever tell your child, "I'll explain that to you when you are older." If they are old enough to ask the question, they are old enough for an answer! If you provide reliable, calm, non-judgmental answers, your kids will learn to bring their questions to you. If you put them off or overreact, then they will learn to ask Google or their peers— which is *not* where you want them to be getting their understanding of the world. Telling your children that they are not ready to know something is a surefire way to close down future important communication. Have you made mistakes in your life? When appropriate, share those with your kids. Why should they have to suffer the same fate just because you didn't want to be open with them? We will talk more about sharing your experiences in chapter 5.

Giving Age-Appropriate Answers

In order to have the most influence on your children, you should always be ready to answer their questions with age-appropriate answers. But what does age-appropriate mean? You will have to determine that based on the maturity of the child. The following guidelines may help.

1. Clarify what they are asking.

2. Try to discern the reason for the question.

3. Only provide as much information as is appropriate.

4. Try to get to the principle that needs to be taught around the issue.

5. Never lie!

It is important to realize that **your child may not necessarily be looking for information, but instead seeking a dialog to expand or explore their own thoughts on a topic.** Often your best response to a question is simply to ask them, "What do *you* think?" This will help turn their question into a conversation. The purpose of asking your own question is to determine the motivation for their inquiry in the first place, because understanding the motivation will determine what kind of answer to give them.

For example, one young son asked his father, "Where do we come from?" His father was surprised to get the question so early, but he understood that this time would eventually come. So he sat his son down and gently explained the birds and the bees. His son listened intently and silently. When the father was finished, the son replied, "The Johnsons come from South Carolina. Where do we come from?"

We can laugh at that story, but the point is for us to answer the questions our children are asking and not add more than they are ready for. Use your own questions to let your child guide you as to how much depth they want.

Your job is to help your children explore their thoughts and feelings and to provide guidance into proper values. While you should provide straightforward answers, you might also use questions to get to a more expanded answer that you know they will need later when they encounter the issue with friends. It is important to explain the principle behind your answers and *why* you believe what you do so that they can defend their beliefs when challenged by others.

It is also important to remember that not all questions have the same importance. Some inquiries are not necessarily something a child is struggling with, but might simply be an extension of a conversation he or she has had at school. In addition, kids are often trying to figure out who they are. They may just be looking for affirmation of your family values. They may be trying to figure out why your family behaves the way you do. These conversations give you a chance to share your worldview, your heritage, and your religious beliefs with your child in a non-threatening way.

When a young child asks where babies come from, he is trying to figure out the basics: Is a baby something you buy? Does it just show up? Do you plan for it? He might be asking because he wants another sibling. Or it might be because he wants to *avoid* getting another brother or sister. When an older child asks, she is probably looking for more specifics. In any case, the real issue is often related to their own identity. Use gentle questions to find out their motivation before answering.

Finally, remember that the ongoing conversation is what is important. You want your child coming back to you again and again to discuss the big issues in life. If you are not comfortable talking about these things yourself, you may need to practice. Try talking with your spouse or even role-playing through some of it. If you show your child that you are uncomfortable talking about something, they will quickly learn to ask someone else. But if you keep an *honest,* open dialog about any issue that might come up, you will have the greatest chance to help your child grow into a positive, healthy adult.

Speaking Truth into Your Kids' Lives

One more word on communication: your kids are longing for parental approval. They need to hear positive things from you constantly. There is an old rule of thumb that a person needs ten positive comments for every negative one, and that statistic is probably too low. Our 21-year-old still brings up some careless negative remarks we made when she was ten.

Kids want to know that you believe in them, and they are skeptically looking for reasons to think you don't. When our kids were in grade school, I thought it would be fun to make a game of one of their Christmas presents. So instead of having a small present in their stockings as is our tradition, I had a clue that would lead them on a little scavenger hunt to find the present. Our two boys thought this was great and eagerly scoured the house for clues and for their presents. If they didn't understand a clue immediately, they pondered it or turned to each other for help. Our daughter, on the other hand, did not appreciate this game. When she could not figure out one of the clues, she crumpled into a sobbing heap, and Christmas was nearly ruined.

What I didn't realize was the message our daughter would get out of that game. Because she couldn't figure out the clue, she felt stupid. Worse, because I expected her to figure it out, it made her feel like she was a disappointment to me. Of course, we did not realize the extent of this emotional damage at the time. We simply revealed her present and Christmas went on—with my wife scolding me for creating the dumb game in the first place. It wasn't until over eight years later that our daughter revealed how that game had hurt her self-image and how she still thinks about it. Talk about feeling set up! Yes, parents, you are going to make mistakes. (See the epilogue for more on that subject.)

The point here is that kids are desperate to know that you approve of them, and they need to hear it constantly and convincingly. It is not enough to tell them they are handsome or pretty or smart. They need specific strengths called out and encouraged. For example, our daughter is one of the most compassionate people you will ever meet. She was constantly defending the other kids at school and watching out for the outcasts. When the tragedy of 9/11 unfolded and America was on the hunt for Osama Bin Laden, she began praying for him.

She did not want him killed; she wanted him healed of his hatred and anger. We could see this positive trait in our daughter and therefore have sought to encourage it in her. We told her we appreciate how she cares for others, and we took the opportunity to tell her it was a very compassionate heart that could pray for the enemy of her country.

Look for truths you can encourage in your children. But be careful that your praise is not all performance-based. Most of your encouragement should be about character. It is less important for you to tell your son he is great at soccer; it is more important to tell him you are impressed with all the hard work he puts in to prepare for each game. As we said earlier, our youngest son is very good at chess (he's a state champion, in fact), and we are very proud of him for that. However, one of the traits we call out in him is what a great sportsman he is. He does not look at his opponents as enemies. He will joke with them and often shares strategies with them after a game. He is concerned not only about winning, but that everyone has a good time, including the people he is playing against. That is something to call out and strengthen in his character.

If your child feels appreciated for who she is and who she is becoming, she is much more likely to be open to other things you have to say, even if those are more critical.

To build communication with your child, you need to build a relationship with him by showing interest in what he is interested in, by getting to know him as a person, and by fostering an environment of open, honest communication that allows your child to ask you anything without you overreacting.

NEXT STEPS:

- Find at least one thing that your child is passionate about, and start making that your interest as well.

- Look for positive traits you can encourage in your kids.

| Crime and Punishment |

"A rod and a reprimand impart wisdom,
but a child left undisciplined disgraces his mother."

A PROVERB OF SOLOMON

As a parent, one of your jobs is to teach your children appropriate behavior. It starts when they are babies and you teach them not to put their fingers into wall outlets, and it continues through their teen years when you make sure they do their homework and don't keep everyone else up at night.

It may not always seem obvious, but disciplining your children is one of the greatest kindnesses you can do for them. They need to learn what is appropriate behavior and what is not, and they need to learn that there are consequences to their actions. If you don't teach them these things in a loving, controlled home environment, then they may get into a lot more trouble later in life when they don't know how to interact with others or control themselves. **If you love your child, you will discipline him. If you do not discipline your child, you are contributing to his possible failure in life.** For the benefit of your children, you need to take control of your home. To do that, you need to set rules and enforce those rules on an ongoing basis.

BBH Principle #3

If you love your child,
you will discipline him.
If you do not discipline your child,
you are contributing to his
possible failure in life.

Sometimes kids actively work against your efforts to bring order to their lives. They don't want to have limits and rules. And their greatest weapon in the fight against discipline is to simply wear you down. Often, they will keep pushing until you give up and give in.

Fortunately, the solution to this problem is simple, but it is not easy. In order for your kids to obey you every time, they need to know that there are definite consequences to their actions. Success in this area is all about follow through. You have to do what you say you are going to do. If you say, "Do that one more time, and I will turn this car around," then when they do it one more time you *have to* turn the car around. If your kids know your threats are meaningless, they will learn to ignore you.

The key is this: **don't ever threaten something you are not willing to do, and don't ever promise something you can't guarantee.** Although it may seem counterintuitive, kids are looking for absolutes—because absolutes provide security. Have you ever driven past a field of horses and noticed how they hang out near the fence? The horses have a huge field to wander in, and yet you will almost always find them right next to the fence. Why is that? Because the fence provides security. It is one less direction from which they can be attacked. Your kids are looking for fences as well, even if they don't realize it. That means that they will keep pushing you until they find the point where you say, "Enough. No further!" They are looking for the security of the boundaries.

In his book *Have a New Kid by Friday*, Dr. Kevin Leman recommends that you only speak any command to your children once. He says, "If you want your child to take you seriously, say your words once. Only once. If you say it more than once, you're implying, 'I think you're so stupid that you're not going to get it the first time, so let me tell you again.'"[1]

This is good advice. By making you repeat yourself, your kids are taking control of the situation. It is a small way of rebelling—of saying, "You're not the boss of me!" And you will be amazed at the immediate results when you stop putting up with that.

"But," you say, "if I don't repeat it, they won't do it." The kids have taught you to think that way. **They aren't going to obey because you repeat the command. They will obey when the consequences of not obeying are worse than the consequences of obeying.**

BBH Principle #4

Don't ever threaten something you are not willing to do, and don't ever promise something you can't guarantee.

What the consequences are depends on the age of the child and the severity of the offense. For older children, the consequence might be the loss of a privilege of some kind—no TV, no video games, no computer, they can't go out with friends, or one of the ultimate penalties in our house: they have to ride the bus to school instead of driving or being driven. Even younger children can lose a special snack or a planned trip to the movies. However, you have to be careful about canceling something you promised, because the kids might see that as you trying to get out of spending time with them instead of it being a consequence of their actions.

For younger children, the consequence has to be immediate. A four-year-old can't compute that he doesn't get a special treat today because he did something bad yesterday. The consequence is too far removed from the crime. Standing in the corner or being put into time-out is a popular consequence for young children.

Punishment vs. Discipline

One quick side note on the term "punishment": There are those who argue that we should never punish our children, but instead we should discipline them. The difference is that punishment is focused on repaying a deed from the past, while discipline is focused on the betterment of the individual for the future. We agree with this distinction. There is no reason to punish your children if you don't care about their future. The whole point of rules and consequences is to craft your child into a well-formed adult who is ready to take their place in society. However, because we like the vernacular of "crime and punishment," and because we think it better captures the importance of teaching children that there are consequences for their actions, we continue to use the terms interchangeably. In any case, everything you do for and to your child should be for the good of that child and the whole family.

Principles for Discipline

As parents, it will be up to you to decide what the consequences are for your children's actions. Below are some guidelines to help you as you determine what is best for your family.

1. **Rules should be known in advance.**

   It is not fair to punish a child for something they did not know was a crime before they committed it. This does not mean that you have to become legalistic and spell everything out. Many things are covered by, "be kind to others." But if you have a problem child, you might need to be more specific. When our oldest child was struggling a little as a young adult, we wrote out a set of guidelines for him and had him sign them. We didn't want any misunderstanding of what was expected of him, and it gave us the opportunity to discuss with him the principles behind each of our rules.

2. **Consequences should be spelled out in advance.**

   If your punishment is random, then it will not be an effective lesson for your kids. If you are speeding, you know that the consequences are that you might get a speeding ticket. The judge is not allowed to put you in jail for a year for speeding. There are appropriate consequences based on the level of the crime, and they are known in advance. This should be true in your house as well.

   One summer our niece and nephew were living with us for a couple of months. They quickly learned that the consequence of breaking our rules was standing in the corner. At one point our niece made our young nephew really angry. We saw him think about it for a minute and then slug her. Then, without saying a word, he went and put himself in the corner. He had decided that the consequence was worth the crime. Of course it made us laugh, but they were learning the valuable life lesson that there are consequences to actions. If the consequences are random, then kids won't respect them, and they (and you) will be frustrated.

3. **The punishment should fit the crime.**
In some families, what ends up happening is that the punishment is determined by how angry Mom or Dad is instead of what the particular crime was. If Dad overlooks an offense four or five times and then suddenly goes ballistic, the child does not learn consequences, he just learns that Dad is overstressed at work—or a little crazy.

4. **Motive should be taken into account.**
Even in criminal courts, the sentence for a crime can depend on the perpetrator's intent. If you accidentally hit someone with your car, you might be charged with manslaughter or you might not be charged at all. But if you purposefully run down the person who took your parking space, then you are going to be charged with murder. In the same way, if your son trips and spills milk on his sister, the punishment should be different than if he purposefully pours it on her. Now, if you had warned him not to carry the milk or if there was a standing rule about that, then he might still be punished for having ignored your directive ... but not for actually spilling the milk on his sister. (She's likely to punish him herself when you aren't looking anyway.)

5. **Only threaten a consequence you will actually follow through on.**
Don't ground your teenager for two weeks if after a couple of days you're not going to remember that you grounded him. Don't ground a child from TV if you are then going to let him

watch it because the other kids will drive you crazy if you turn it off. This is important. If you learn nothing else from this chapter, apply this: **Your threatened discipline MUST be carried out.** Of course, you might shorten a sentence for good behavior, but it has to be for a good reason, not just because the consequences became inconvenient to you or the rest of the family.

6. **Take the pain.**

Kids quickly pick up on fake threats. If you say, "do that again, and we are going home right now," you better be prepared to go home right then. We recently traveled with another family to Disney World. We explained the rules to all the kids when we got there. And we explained the consequence of breaking the rules: they would miss out on the current activity, and if they were particularly bad, one of us would take them back to the hotel, where they could sit out of the fun for the day. That may seem harsh, but it is better for your child over the long-term to miss a day at Disney if it means he only has to learn the lesson once. Of course, that means at least one of the parents has to miss the day as well. Parenting can often be sacrificial—that's just part of the job. Remember that your child's growth is more important than the current activity—even if that activity happens to be a movie or dinner out or even Disney World. Occasionally you will run into the quandary that to punish one child affects the others. If you cancel a trip to McDonalds because two of the kids are fighting, that affects everyone. Yes, disobedience affects the entire family! This is a good lesson for the other children. What they do doesn't just affect them. Occasionally you might go ahead and get something for the "good" kids, but at other times you need to just let them all suffer—including you. You can also teach children self-sacrifice by imposing a restriction on yourself to help a child. For instance, if TV is really keeping one of your kids from getting their homework done, maybe the TV doesn't get turned on at all until all the homework is done. And that includes for *you*. Being part of a family means that sometimes the good of the one outweighs the good of the many.

7. **Don't be vindictive.**
    Once the child has served his time, don't bring it up again or wave it in his face. Kids need to learn that there are consequences, but there is also healing. When our children were young, we applied spanking when necessary. (See *Guidelines on Corporal Punishment* later in this chapter.) But the parent who did the spanking was also the one to console the child afterwards. We always explained to them that we did this because we wanted them to grow up to be healthy, happy people, and for that to happen, they needed to learn not to do what they had done. Kids are smart. They "get it" when punishment is doled out consistently and in love. Withholding love should never be part of the punishment. You should always try to make it clear to your child that you love him, even when your role as a parent requires you to punish him.

8. **Try not to punish in anger.**
    Punishment should be a result of the child breaking a rule, not the result of him making you angry. If you can't dole out the consequence in a non-prejudiced way, then you need to recuse yourself from being the judge. Sometimes you might

need to just calm down first and then handle the situation, or you might need to get your spouse to handle it. However, you have to be careful not to make your spouse the bad guy all the time. Don't resort to the "Wait till your father gets home" speech. Do you really want to teach your children that Dad coming home is a bad thing? And do you think that is what Dad wants to come home to?

9. **Set punishments your spouse will uphold.**
   It is vital that you and your spouse are a team when it comes to parenting. You already know that kids will divide and conquer when they are trying to get something they want. We will discuss this more later, but for now, it is important that you work with your spouse to agree on the consequence-levels together. For example, you don't want Dad to say "no TV for a week" if Mom is going to ignore that as soon as Dad goes to work because she needs the child to be entertained while she gets her work done. And you don't want Mom to say, "You can't go on that trip with your Dad," if Dad doesn't agree and is going to take the child anyway. One of the stresses of marriage is that we assume the other parent has the same parenting standards. But you had different parents and different family experiences growing up, so your standards are unlikely to match in every regard. It can really help to intentionally sit down with your spouse and discuss which punishments you will use for what levels of crime and agree in advance to uphold each other's decrees.

10. Don't veto your spouse in front of your children.

There are times when you won't agree on your spouse's choice of punishment. You might think that the consequences are too severe or are not severe enough. That is fine. You are a team, and you are supposed to help each other figure this parenting thing out. However, it is really important that your kids see you as a unified force. If Dad doesn't agree with a punishment Mom has given out, he needs to keep his mouth shut until he can talk to Mom alone and then he can argue his case as to why he thinks his daughter should still be allowed to go to the party. If you do decide together to change the punishment, make sure that the parent who gave out the punishment is also the one who announces the change. Otherwise, kids will quickly learn that they can pit one parent against the other or that they can ignore punishment from one parent because the other will always bail them out. And that is a bad situation for your family, for your child, and for your marriage.

11. Consider involving the family.

One principle you should strive to teach your children is that each person's actions affect the group. For example, if you decide to turn the TV off for a few days because of one child's transgressions, everyone is affected. And that is okay. They need to learn that they don't live in isolation. The actions of one individual in society do affect the rest of us.

When our kids were old enough, we would sometimes get their input on what they thought the punishment should be. Often, we would ask the offender, "You know you shouldn't have done this. How do you think we should punish you?" And they almost always were more severe than we would have been! If a crime particularly affected the whole family, then we might ask the other kids what they thought the punishment should be. For example, when one of our children was consistently refusing to do his homework, we threatened that if he didn't start doing it, then he wouldn't get to come with us on our upcoming trip to Florida. Well, he didn't do it, and we were forced to follow up on our threat. (Remember BBH Principle #4: never threaten what you are not willing to do!) However, when we announced this to the other children, they felt that his absence would affect the rest of the family too much, and they suggested an alternative punishment for him, which was severe but would allow us to still have the trip as a family. Because the alternative came from the rest of the family and not from the offender or the parents, our trip was saved and the kids learned a valuable lesson about working as a group.

12. **Give your child the benefit of the doubt.**
Don't assume that they will commit an offense until they actually have. We recently overheard a family's conversation in a restaurant. The daughter asked, "What time is the Luau?" The dad responded by berating her for always planning something else. Maybe she was, but his response assumed the worst. There was nothing wrong with the question. Only punish your child when an offense actually takes place. Would you want someone reading your thoughts and attacking you every time you thought something you shouldn't? If you can tell a child is thinking something mean, but she refrained from saying it, she is learning an important lesson about when to stay silent. Don't be the thought police.

13. Each child is different.

A common trap that parents fall into is to try to have one set of rules and consequences for all their children. Each child is different. Their motives are different, their actions are different, and their thoughts are different. What will help one child grow into a healthy, well-formed adult won't be the same as what will help another child. For example, when it came to disciplining our children, we had to take different tacks. To punish our daughter, all we had to do was to tell her that we were disappointed in her, and that was enough to upset her and change her behavior. Our oldest son, on the other hand, was very difficult to punish because he would simply accept whatever condition we tried to place on him. Make him stand in the corner? Okay, he likes the alone time. Make him ride the bus instead of driving his car? Okay, that's fine. And to really drive his parents insane, when he was little he once asked Mom to spank him even though he hadn't done anything wrong. This is what is called psychological warfare. In any case, you will need to figure out what is best for each child, which includes both the rules and the consequences. If a child is more responsible, give him more freedom even if the other kids don't get that same privilege. It is a valuable life lesson for all of them that their personal responsibility provides them greater freedom.

14. Where appropriate, apply rules to yourself.

Kids are watching you to see if you walk the talk and believe what you are teaching, so they need to see that you hold yourself to similar standards. Lisa used to be pretty bad about putting on her seat belt, which of course we require the children to do. So she empowered the children. She told them that every time they caught her not wearing her seat belt, they could charge her a dollar. This was good for her, since she was more likely to wear her seat belt, but it was also good for them as they saw that rules applied to Mom and Dad as well.

Of course, not all the same rules will apply to you that apply to your children. For example, you might have a rule that the kids can't watch TV after 7 p.m. on a school night, but you can. It is fine to have separate rules, just remember that it is the principles you are trying to teach them, so you better have a good "why" for the difference other than just, "because I am the parent." Kids are always looking to see if you really believe what you teach. When your actions don't match up—like if you smoke but tell your kids not to smoke—they are less likely to listen to you about other things.

15. Give children control of their fate.

When kids are young they need rules, but as quickly as possible, you should transition toward the application of principles. The goal is to teach them to be good decision makers on their own, and for that to happen they have to have a chance to make decisions and experience the consequences. One of the things we did as our children got older was to give them more control over their schooling. For example, if they wanted to take a day off, they could. As long as their grades were good, we left them in charge of their education. If their grades dipped, then they lost that privilege. What did this teach them? That positive actions give them greater control over their lives and greater freedom—a principle that is true in all of life. You might not want to start with something as large as school days, but the idea is to look for areas where you can give your kids control of their fate and they can experience the consequences. Just remember not to bail them out if their choices lead to bad consequences. They need to learn that lesson as well.

16. Don't be afraid to apologize.

You are going to make mistakes. You will discipline when you shouldn't have. When our oldest son was about three or four we went to JCPenney for a shopping trip. As Mom pushed our younger daughter through the store in a stroller, our daughter reached out and grabbed some sweaters, knocking the whole stack on the floor. Our son started picking up the sweaters and putting them back. Mom turned around and "caught him red handed" messing with the sweaters, and he got in trouble. Fortunately, I was following them and saw the whole thing, so I could tell Mom what really happened. When you make a mistake, don't give the, "well it's the kind of thing you would do" speech. Just apologize. Kids need to hear their parents apologize to each other and to them. Don't worry; it won't undercut your authority. Just the opposite, it will model a fairness and gentleness that will make them much more likely to listen to you in the future.

The Five C's

The above principles may be a little too much to grasp all at once, so here is a simplified version that we call the Five C's. If you begin by applying these, you will see a big difference in your family.

1. **Consequences**

   One of the most important lessons you can teach your children is that there are consequences to their behavior and their choices.

2. **Clarity**

   Kids need to know the rules and the consequences. You might consider putting them in writing. Spelling them out will provide clarity for the kids, for your spouse, and for you. Having your rules and consequences spelled out in advance will also help you to not react emotionally when the kids do something they shouldn't. Your kids should understand the reasons for your rules as much as possible.

3. **Consistency**

   Upholding the rules consistently will teach the kids fairness—a very important life lesson. Consistency doesn't mean that the same rules apply to everyone (you might decide that teenagers can stay up until 10 p.m., but younger kids have to go to bed at 9 p.m.), but that the rules for each child are applied consistently.

4. **Coordination with Spouse**

   Discipline is much more effective if both parents uphold the rules and the consequences, so try to agree on them before disciplining the kids.

5. **Control**

   Give children control of their fate as much as possible in order for them to really learn how to apply the life principles you are trying to teach.

Guidelines on Corporal Punishment

King Solomon was considered the wisest man who ever lived, and his ages-old advice on parenting is, "If you spare the rod, you will spoil the child." This advice has created great debate within modern parenting circles because many people envision an angry parent slapping or hitting their child. Such actions, of course, are not the appropriate use of corporal punishment. All discipline should be done in love, not in anger, for the purpose of training your child up in the way she should go.

The point of Solomon's advice is not that you must spank your child, but instead that in order for children to grow into healthy adults, they need to experience real, painful consequences for bad behavior. In most cases, you can provide this consequence without it being physical punishment. In fact, due to the rise of child abuse, or at least the awareness of child abuse, many child professionals have eschewed spanking, and corporal punishment has been outlawed in 30 countries[2]. So if you can effectively use an alternate consequence, then use that instead.

Remember that each child is different. Some just need time-outs, some just need to be told you are disappointed with them, but others aren't going to get the lesson unless there is appropriate pain involved. Better a little pain now than a lifetime of dangerous behavior. Whether you use spanking or not, you should be looking for the most appropriate way to discipline each of your children in order to raise them to be healthy adults.

For parents who determine that a particular child needs loving physical discipline, we offer the following guidelines.

- **Never in anger**

  The purpose of all discipline is to help the child. If you cannot discipline your child without being angry or vindictive, then please don't use spanking. In fact, unless you are certain you can use corporal punishment correctly and lovingly, or if you are concerned that it might harm your child, you should not do it.

- **Corporal punishment is for the young**

  If you are trying to teach a toddler not to touch a hot stove or stick his finger in an electrical outlet, it is appropriate to spank his hand. He is too young to understand a reasonable explanation, and pain is the body's way of learning not to repeat the same action. However, as quickly as possible, you should transition to consequences other than corporal punishment. As children get older, there are much more effective means for getting their attention. Basically, you find out what they like and withhold it for a set time.

- **Only on the fleshy parts**

  Corporal punishment is meant to provide a painful lesson so that your children learn. It is not mean to harm your child. So if you are going to spank your child, it should be on the bottom, not on the face, arms, legs, etc. The only exception to this is that you might swat or flick a very young child's hands as you say, "No!" to show him not to touch something that will harm him (like putting his fingers into an electrical outlet). In cases like that, spanking his bottom is too far removed from the act of reaching out for the dangerous item.

- **Always explain the why**

  Many of us got the speech from our parents that "this is going to hurt me worse than it hurts you." That is a terrible speech. It doesn't convince kids, it just confuses them. However, you should always explain why you are disciplining a child. Discipline, especially corporal punishment, should never be a surprise. It should be the expected result of willful misconduct on the part of the child breaking a known and understood rule. (Like getting a traffic ticket when you choose to speed.) I remember telling our kids, "I hate punishing you. I hate it! But my job is to help you grow up to be the best person you can be. And because I care about you, you have to learn this lesson." Our children understood. And I think it was a strong testimony to the love with which we administered spankings that the kids would always come back to the spanking parent to be held and comforted after the punishment was over.

- **Infrequent**

  If you find yourself spanking your child more than a couple of times per month, it is probably not an effective training tool for that child, and you should try something else, like time-outs, standing in the corner, grounding, etc.

- **Final warning on spanking**

  Even if you are a loving parent who is appropriately using spanking to discipline your child, you can still end up in trouble with the authorities. If someone sees you spanking your child in public, or if they see a red mark on the child's bottom, they can anonymously report you for possible child abuse. Your children may be snatched away from you and subjected to terrifying interrogation by child protective services. So while we encourage you to discipline your children, be sure that spanking is really the only choice for that child.

Setting the Rules

Now that we have covered the principles of family crime and punishment, it is time to set your own rules. To do this, think about what will make your kids into healthy adults. When Lisa and I were first married, we sat down and talked about the traditions and rules we had grown up with that we liked. We chose the best from both families and added our own.

The goal is to teach your kids principles to live by. You start with rules, but as the kids learn the "whys" of those rules, the rules become less important. For example, we started with a rule of no R-rated movies, with the "why" being that what you watch fills your mind and affects who you are. We taught the kids that images from movies affect their dreams, their fears, and their life choices. Movies are like food for our minds—and some can be poisonous. As they grew older, we no longer had a hard-and-fast rule about movie ratings, but instead, the kids had to be able to explain to us how a particular film would be a positive addition to their lives.

A few years ago, some family friends of ours moved away, but their college-age daughter wanted to stay and finish school, so she moved in with us. She went to the two kids we still had at home and asked them what our family rules were. The kids had to think about it for a long time. We had long since transitioned to principles, so we didn't really have any set rules, per se. They weren't necessary anymore. The kids finally came up with our basic family rule: no lying! In our house, lying is considered the worst offense because it breaks the relationship. You and your spouse will have to come up with what your own rules are and what the principles behind those rules are.

Pick Your Battles

As you determine your family rules and the consequences for breaking those rules, we want to caution you to pick your battles carefully. It is not important for you to control your child in every circumstance. It is more important to *direct* him. Remember that the goal is to prepare him to take his place in society without you, which means that he needs to learn to make good decisions. How does one learn to make good decisions? By making bad ones!

You certainly want to keep your child away from drugs, but is it really important to keep him from getting a pierced ear? What life lesson are you teaching by fighting that battle? I remember when our teenage son announced that he wanted to get his ears pierced. "Okay," Mom said, "I'll take you." His response? "Never mind." He was just trying to get a rise out of us. When we didn't react, it wasn't important anymore. Another time, he decided he wanted blue hair, so his Mom took him to her salon, where they first bleached his brown hair to blond so that the blue dye would work. By not fighting the small things, we have a much greater influence when something is truly important. When our oldest son was a teenager, he decided to let his hair grow really long. We did not try to stop him, although we did laugh when people called him Ma'am. On the other hand, we did require him to take care of it, and we often told our children that personal appearance does affect their job opportunities. Some hairstyles, piercings, etc. say "please don't employ me."

You will need to decide which hills are worth dying on. Just remember that it shouldn't be about what *your* friends will say about *you* when they see your kid with blue hair. It should be about what is best for him as he figures out how to be an adult.

It is not necessary to address every infraction. For example, sometimes you need to confront a nasty attitude, but other times it is okay to let a child stew. Your job is to prepare your children for life, not to be the thought police. You will need to decide based on each child's behavior and personality how often you need to reinforce a lesson and how often you can let them have their own thoughts and emotions. Also, keep external factors in mind. One thing Lisa has been better at than I is recognizing when the kids are acting poorly because they are tired or hungry or out of their element. Sometimes they just need some patience and grace.

A Final Word on Hypocrisy

As you take charge of your kids and begin to apply consistent rules to them, you are going to hear the dreaded words, "You're such a hypocrite!" Kids will say this to try to discount advice that you give them when they know you are imperfect. We have the answer for you. This alone is worth the price of this book! Let's say that you are extolling to your teenage daughter the woes of sleeping with her boyfriend before marriage, and she points out that you were not so saintly before you were married. Ask her, "If you touch a pot and burn yourself, shouldn't you warn the next person not to touch the same pot?" Your job is to help your kids grow to be positive adults so they can enjoy life. Yes, you have made mistakes, and the last thing you want is for your kids to repeat the same mistakes. Those mistakes brought pain and misery and consequences that you have had to live with.

Of course, lessons don't have to be so dramatic, either. Perhaps you are simply telling your child to have patience and they point out that you lose your temper a lot. Again, you can talk about how that weakness causes problems for you and how you want a better start for them. We often tell our kids, "Well, you have better parents than we did."

Why should your kids have to repeat your mistakes or the mistakes of your parents? Just setting rules won't break that cycle; you will need to be honest with them about your poor choices and the results of those choices. Through loving, humble transparency, you have a chance to raise better children and change your family's legacy.

Warning your children of the dangers of bad choices you made is not hypocrisy. It is common decency.

NEXT STEPS:

- Work with your spouse to determine what your house rules are and what the consequences are for breaking those rules.

- Communicate the rules and consequences to the kids and tell them that you are setting those rules to help them grow to be positive adults.

- Be open to discussion and negotiation during rule setting with both your spouse and your kids, but try to avoid negotiation with the kids when you are applying the rules that have already been agreed to.

CHAPTER 4

The Importance of Social Skills

"Through patience a ruler can be persuaded,
and a gentle tongue can break a bone."

A PROVERB OF SOLOMON

Every generation complains that kids don't have any manners. But today it seems like some parents may have lost sight of the importance of social skills altogether. They think of things like salad forks and folded napkins and fail to see how those can possibly benefit their children. But imparting social skills to our children not only prepares them for life's social situations, it can also teach them how to be gracious and how to respect others and themselves. Well-mannered adults are more likely to get and keep a good job, are more likely to attract and keep a loving spouse, and are generally more enjoyable to be around.

On a recent business trip, we observed a mom with two small children waiting to board a Southwest flight. The two boys did *not* want to get onto the plane, and they continued to tell their mother this as boarding time approached. She reassured them that it would be all right and just kept on waiting. When it was actually time to board and the kids started down the jetway, the rest of the passengers were both amused and touched to hear the youngest one say, "No thank you, please. No thank you, please," over and over again. He did not want to get on the plane, and his well-mannered response was quite touching. In fact, when the pilot overheard the child's plea, he came out and invited both children into the cockpit. He showed them around, and suddenly the children's experience went from fear to wonder. Do you think the captain would have invited those children into the cockpit if they had been screaming? Their manners made the entire situation more positive. Those parents were doing a good job.

BBH Principle #5

Social skills help children learn that they are not the center of the universe and that their actions can have a positive or negative impact on others.

Social skills help children learn that they are not the center of the universe and that what they say and do can have a positive or negative impact on others.

Here are some basic social skills you might want to consider imparting to your children:

Gratitude

Teaching your children to have a heart of gratitude will make them more pleasant to be around, will help them to lead a happier life, and can benefit all of their interpersonal relationships[3]. For many parents, teaching gratitude starts and stops with teaching children to say thank you when they are given something. But true gratitude means looking for opportunities to acknowledge other people and having an appreciation of everything that has been provided. You can start by teaching your children to appreciate your spouse. That means making sure they do special things for Mom on Mother's Day and her birthday and Christmas and Easter and Valentine's Day and Thanksgiving and other times throughout the year. Teach your children how to select an appropriate gift and don't just buy it for them … make them part of the process to select it and preferably pay for it. If Mom appreciates handmade things, then they can make her a card or write her a poem. The key is to teach them to do something Mom will like, not something that is easy. On my wife's birthday, she sends flowers to *her* mother to thank her for bringing her into this world. And now our daughter has started doing this same thing for her mother. Teach your children to use effort and creativity to show appreciation. Their future spouse will thank you for raising them right.

It is important to teach your children how to give good, thoughtful gifts, but it is also important to teach them how to receive a gift graciously. Through both words and modeling, you can teach your children to acknowledge any gift they are given and the effort of the giver. When I was growing up, my family celebrated Christmas in a mad dash to open all the presents at once. By doing it that way, we were taught that Christmas was all about what we could get—we didn't really pay any attention to who the giver was. Lisa and I chose a different way to handle presents. We require the children to take their time. Only one person opens a present at a time, and we go around the room with everyone watching as each gift is opened. This causes the receiver to acknowledge the giver, and the giver hears everyone in the family comment on the gift. Not only does this approach result in a far more peaceful Christmas, but the kids quickly come to enjoy being the giver even more than the receiver.

Another aspect of gratitude is appreciating what your whole family has. Have you ever heard the phrase, "seeing how the other half lives"? Isn't it interesting that no matter how well off we are, the "other half" is always people who have *more* than we have? The truth is that if you live in America, the other half of the world is nowhere near as well off as you are. Do your kids know that? Do they hear you being appreciative for what you have, or do they just hear you always wishing you had more? We had the unusual opportunity to take our children to Africa when they were grade school/middle school age. What they saw there permanently changed their perspective on what they have and made them appreciate how blessed they are. While you may not be able to go to Africa, you can certainly visit those less fortunate than you to truly show your kids how "the other half" lives. If possible, you should take your kids and volunteer for an organization that helps the poor. This will help them learn gratitude and service. These kinds of lessons take time, but they are not difficult. Think of ways you can intentionally make your family more grateful.

Patience

Patience may be one of the true victims of our modern age. Everything is instant. We live in a wonderful society where we can get whatever we want whenever we want it, regardless of season or location. We can travel long distances instantly, we can cook instantly, and we can get information instantly. Our kids rarely have to wait, and waiting is definitely a skill that is learned. Movies show training montages where the main characters become experts at something in a few short screen moments. Video games allow kids to be great at many things without practice. But more than all of these contributing factors, our kids are not patient because we don't require it of them. We have lost the fine art of just waiting.

The Fine Art of Waiting

Kids need to learn the art of conversation, the practice of waiting patiently on others, and being fully present with others even when the activity at hand is not interesting to them. It is important for children to learn that life does not always revolve around them. If Mom is not done eating her dinner, the kids can sit quietly and wait or, better, remain involved in the family discussion until everyone is finished. And waiting does not mean playing on an iPhone or watching a movie on an iPad. It does not include looking exasperated or rolling their eyes. It means remaining engaged in the conversation until everyone is done. The first few times you enforce this might be a battle, but the trick is to make their bad behavior very painful to them so they learn for the future. If you let your kids hide behind technology or, worse, get up and wander around the restaurant or wait outside, you are teaching them that they are more important than their mother, and you are actively making them into boring individuals who do not know how to interact in society.

Want peace and quiet at dinner? Get a babysitter and go out by yourselves or go somewhere like McDonalds or Chuck E. Cheese where the kids can run off and play while you sit and talk. However, if you want your children to grow to be well-rounded adults, you need to take time for intentional family dinner outings where kids learn what is expected of them. And in the spirit of good communication, we suggest spelling out up front what your expectations are. Before going into the restaurant, tell the kids that they are expected to sit quietly and pleasantly until everyone is finished with their meal. And tell them the consequences if they do not—something you will actually follow through on! Do *not* promise a reward if they sit quietly. It is not some favor they are doing you. They need to learn that good manners are expected. Now, if your kids are particularly well behaved (or even if only some of them are), be sure to praise that behavior afterwards and feel free to reward it with something special. But they should be behaving because of your request and because it is right, not because of a promised reward. If you have not yet practiced this with your kids, then start by going somewhere where your meal will be short and work your way up to something longer. The earlier you teach your children this skill, the better.

You can even start this lesson at home. When our daughter was young, she had a lot of trouble staying in her chair during dinner. She would get up and run around the dining room while the rest of us were still eating. No amount of threats would keep her in her chair. She did not intend to be defiant; she just didn't have a long attention span. So we resorted to using a homemade seat belt to keep her in her chair. She is now 21 and is a wonderful companion at any meal, but we still joke about her 4-year-old seat belts.

Your kids can learn appropriate social behavior even at a young age. Don't say, "But she is only four, and it is cute." Will it still be cute when she is 13 and won't sit with you at dinner? It is always easier to start early.

Forcing kids to stop and be in the moment may feel difficult when you begin but will become easier as they learn the skill. Learning to be comfortable without outside entertainment will make them calmer, happier individuals who are better able to enjoy life as it comes.

You can teach your children patience by demonstrating the quality yourself and by intentionally discussing it with them. Tell them that patience is a positive attribute and show them when you are practicing patience, like when you are waiting in line for something or are stuck in traffic. You can even go on a patience hunt with them. Ask them to point out to you when you are being impatient, and you can work on cultivating patience together.

Lack of patience often keeps us from enjoying the moment. **We need to teach children to be participants in life rather than consumers of what life has to offer them.** Teach your kids to enjoy the moment and they will never be bored. How do you enjoy the moment? Consider the good things. For example, let's say you decide to go camping and the weather turns bad so you are stuck in the tent. You can either lament that you didn't get to do the hiking and canoeing and other activities you had planned or, instead, you can show your kids that you can be creative and enjoy the moments in the tent: playing cards, telling stories, asking and answering questions, etc. When was the last time you just made up a story on the spot? How about doing a story in the round where you start and then your kids add to the story and you just keep going around with family members putting in ideas to see where the story goes? You can find creative ways to reject impatience and enjoy each moment.

Kindness

We all want to raise kind children. You teach your children to be kind by demonstrating kindness not only to them, but to others, and by requiring them to be kind to their siblings, to their parents, and to everyone they meet. A child with a kind and gracious spirit will be an enjoyment to others and will be better able to enjoy others themselves.

Part of kindness is serving others. Is your child getting up to get a drink for themselves? Remind them to ask their siblings if they want a drink as well. When our children were young, we would have them take turns being the designated waiter at meal time so that Mom didn't have to keep getting up. Not only did the kids learn to serve others, but they enjoyed playing the part.

BBH Principle #6

Use punishment for behavior.
Use reward for attitude.

As you work to teach social skills, you should teach your children that you expect the correct behavior even when they don't feel like it. It is occasionally okay for them to think that something is stupid, as long as they still do it. For example, when you meet your friends at a store, perhaps you will require your children to greet them or even shake their hands. Your kids may not want to do this since they don't know the people. Your children don't always have to agree in order to do the right thing. Understanding that sometimes they just have to suck it up and do what they don't like will serve them well in their jobs later in life.

Once you begin setting clear expectations, you will discover that your children will rise to meet those expectations. However, you may also find that behavior is easier to control than attitude. Much of what we discussed in the last chapter is about setting rules and getting your children to follow those rules. And certainly there are some social rules you want to teach your children; however, the larger social lessons have more to do with attitude and character traits.

One thing that might help is to think of using punishment for behavior and using reward for attitude. You should resist telling children, "be good and you will get a treat." They should be good because you tell them to or, better, because it is the right thing to do, not because of a promised reward or bribe. When you bribe your children to be good, you are letting them be in control. They will learn that they have power over you to get what they want. And when they are in control of the relationship, they are going to lead you down bad parenting paths. Instead, require them to obey you and follow the rules by giving or withholding discipline.

However, you can reward an especially good attitude *after the fact*. For example, let's say the grandparents are coming over to dinner and you tell the kids they have to sit and listen to their grandparents until dinner is over. Don't promise something for good behavior, require it. If they give you a hard time, then there should be grounding or some other consequence for them being rude to their grandparents and ignoring your request. On the other hand, if they sit nicely and interact with their grandparents, then afterwards you can tell them how proud you are of them and even reward them with something special. It is a subtle but important difference. They should obey simply because you asked, not because they expect a reward, but you can reward them for having a great attitude.

As you can see, there are many aspects to teaching your child social skills. It goes way beyond manners and encompasses the correct way to deal with other people in every situation. If your children learn how to appropriately deal with other people even in tough situations, then they will truly be ready for life.

FURTHER SUGGESTED READING:

- *How to Be a Gentleman: A Timely Guide to Timeless Manners* by John Bridges (Thomas Nelson, 2008)

NEXT STEPS:

- Pick a social skill or trait you would like to see in your children and find ways to intentionally work on that trait both privately and publicly.

- Start expecting the best from your kids and begin communicating those expectations.

| Love, Sex, and Marriage |

*"Many waters cannot quench love, nor can rivers drown it.
If a man tried to buy love with all his wealth,
his offer would be utterly scorned."*

SONG OF SOLOMON

*"There is no difference between a wise man
and a fool when they fall in love."*

ANONYMOUS

One of the most exciting parts of growing up is figuring out the opposite sex. From first crush to marriage, the entire experience is an adventure filled with excitement, drama, and often disappointment. Part of your job as a parent is to help guide your kids through the rough seas of love, sex, and marriage (preferably not in that order).

For kids to have a chance at happy, healthy marriages, they have to start with a healthy understanding of the opposite sex. Too many parents focus on the one "sex talk" when their kids are teenagers. But in reality, if you wait too long, most of their attitudes and misconceptions will already be set. However, there is a better, easier, and

simpler way of training up your children to have healthy relationships. It is easiest to begin when they are small, but it is never too
late to start.

The simple secret is the same as we mentioned under
Communication in chapter 2, and that is to foster an environment
where your kids can talk to you about *everything*. You do that by
making it clear to them that no subject is off-limits. In our family,
we often did this at the dinner table, and we might even start with
leading questions to get the conversation going. Kids see what is
happening around them, and they take it all in. It becomes part of
who they are. You will not be able to protect them from life, but you
can help them learn to process life appropriately. For example, let's
say you and your spouse have a fight and the kids hear it. Once the
fight is over and resolved, you can use it as a good opportunity to
teach the kids about love and marriage. "Did you notice Mommy
and Daddy arguing earlier? We want you to know that Mommy and
Daddy love each other very much, and sometimes married people
disagree and argue. It doesn't mean we don't love each other or don't
like each other. Most of our fights are really just miscommunication,
and if we were more patient with each other we would probably have
fewer arguments. Remember that you can ask us anything. Do you
have any questions about this?"

Things that happen in your family or in your extended family or at
their school or even in the news can all be conversation starters. Of
course, for this to work you have to be prepared to be real with your
kids. When we showed this chapter to our 21-year-old daughter, she
added this comment:

> "There were times when if we heard you guys fight-
> ing in an unkind manner, you came to us later and

apologized for treating our mother so ungraciously. That made such an impact on my view of love, repentance, and how our actions affect others."

You can use your weaknesses as opportunities to help point your kids to a better way. Don't think you need to look perfect to your kids—they will find out soon enough that you're not. You will be a more effective parent if you let them see some of your struggles. Not all of them—your kids should not be your counselors or confidants. You should share what is important to *their* growth, not yours. In addition, by showing your children that you have struggles, they will realize that they are not expected to be perfect, which will result in a healthier approach to many of life's problems.

Other than answering their questions, the main way you teach your children about sex is by example. Want your kids to know how to appropriately date and court a person of the opposite sex? Demonstrate appropriate courting with your spouse. For example, don't ever tell your kids that sex is bad. Sex is not bad, it is just meant for marriage. If they know this early on, they are much less likely to struggle with sexual issues. When my oldest son got married, we had a sex talk, but it was not about the birds and the bees, it was about how to please his wife. That is the kind of conversation you can only have if you have spent his lifetime building trust and open communication about any issue.

Do you want your children to dress modestly? Consider how you dress. Again, you want to teach them principles. They need to understand that the other sex is wired differently than they are. If your daughter wears revealing clothes, she is sending a certain signal to boys. Does she *want* to send that signal? My wife would often tell our daughter, "This is what your clothes are communicating. Is that your intention?"

For boys, it is important to teach them the dangers of pornography. This is not going to happen by osmosis. First, Dad needs to avoid pornography himself, but second, he needs to be able to tell his son that pornography opens up all kinds of evil in a man's heart and life and will distort his view of girls and his relationship with his eventual wife. One of the things we stress with all of our kids in discussing both pornography and any kind of entertainment is that images you allow into your mind cannot be erased. The images they expose themselves to will be in their minds forever and will become part of who they are. I can still remember images I saw in college that I wish I had not exposed myself to. They are an unnecessary distraction in my life. Kids need to understand that what they feed their eyes becomes part of who they are. They should be asking themselves, "Do I really want that to be part of what defines me?"

Once you set the expectation that kids can ask you anything, you will be surprised to find out what they think about. You can help mold how your children process information on love, sex, and marriage. If you don't provide input, you

BBH Principle #7

As parents, you can have the greatest impact on your child's healthy view of love, sex, and marriage.

leave it up to their friends, movies, and the Internet. Do these sources represent the worldview you want to pass on to your kids? **The truth is that you, as parents, can have the greatest impact on your child's healthy view of love, sex, and marriage.**

One lesson that we try to teach our children is to show value to the person they are dating by not putting them into a situation that might damage their reputation. It is especially important to teach your sons to guard their girlfriend's reputation. When our son was dating the girl who would eventually become his wife, we talked to them about how they were sitting together on the sofa while watching movies. They would complain that they see us sitting under a blanket or sitting in each other's lap. We explained that we have a license, and we would always point to our wedding rings. There is nothing wrong with snuggling with your spouse. But, we explained to our son, if he was doing this with his girlfriend and they didn't end up getting married, then he was snuggling with someone else's wife, which was not appropriate. In this way, we were teaching them that romance is great in marriage, but that they need to protect themselves and their dating partner until that time.

Of course, in teaching them how to protect their girlfriend or boyfriend, we also need to show them how we protect our marriage. Share with your kids how you guard your marriage. What boundaries do you have? For example, we try to avoid one-on-one meals with our coworkers of the opposite sex. There wouldn't be anything wrong with it, it is just one way of protecting our marriage, and we explain that to our kids. We aren't just putting limits on them, we also put limits on ourselves. Kids will often counter with an angry, "You don't trust me." Lisa would often say to them, "*You* shouldn't trust you." The question to get them to consider is, "Why put yourself in a situation where you might go beyond your pre-determined boundaries?" I once asked a client why he didn't dance with women colleagues at a trade show banquet where everyone was dancing. His response was very wise. He said, "If I never go near the edge of the cliff, I don't need to worry about falling off."[4]

I travel a lot for business, so one way I protect my heart and my marriage is that I put a blanket or towel over the TV in the hotel room to protect myself from the temptation or even accidental exposure to pornography—and my kids know it.

Dating

One of the areas you will need to teach your children about is dating. When should they date? The answer depends on the maturity level of the child. The more important question is *why* they should or should not date. To find a spouse? To explore relationships? To feel loved? So they aren't made fun of at school? To get to know people? Don't be afraid to explore this question with your teenagers who want to date. Help them figure out in their own minds what they are looking for.

Lisa and I are big believers in kids starting with group dating or outings. It is a way to get to know people without the hormonal or social pressures. A group date does not mean two or three couples. A group date or outing is a group of kids most of whom are not dating each other. They can hang out and learn how to interact socially.

When they are ready for individual dating, it is up to you to teach your kids what's appropriate. One of the best ways to do this is to begin dating your children when they are young. This means that Dad takes the daughter out and Mom takes the son out individually by themselves. Dad can teach his daughter how a young man should treat her—even things like dressing nicely and opening doors. Don't you want your daughter to be selective in who she dates and to have high standards? You can help to set those standards.

When it comes time for children to begin actual dating or court-ing, suggest dates that are public and have lots of interaction. A visit to an ice cream shop or a fondue place or even an amusement park is going to teach them a lot more about their friend than a visit to a movie where they don't interact with each other.

Remember, it is not hypocrisy to teach your children the right way to date even if you didn't follow the right path. If you got burned touching a hot pan, it is not hypocrisy to warn others not to touch it—it is common decency.

When your child starts to explore an actual relationship, you can help the young couple build a strong, appropriate relationship by fostering good communication. For example, sit the two of them down and ask them what their boundaries for physical touch are. If they are uncomfortable talking to you about the subject, that is prob-ably a bad sign. Teach them that it is much easier to set boundaries in the light of day than in the heat of the moment. Because we have a culture of communication in our family where no subject is off-limits, we can ask very direct questions: What are your boundaries? Is it holding hands? Is it kissing? Is it petting?

If you want your kids to be real with you, don't assume that their boundaries are going to be what you think they should be. If they express thoughts or plans that you don't agree with, don't immedi-ately react negatively. Otherwise, they will just stop talking to you. You want the chance to help influence their thinking—the chance to be a voice in the discussion they are having. If you don't freak out, you will have more opportunities to guide them, but that means you have to be willing to hear answers that you don't necessarily agree with.

Communication is the key. No subject should be off-limits. And if your kids do mess up, you want them to come to you, not go to some friend or teacher. (See more on *Kids in Crisis* in chapter 8.)

Starting Late

If you want to give your kids a chance at a great marriage, demonstrate how to interact with the opposite sex and show them how to keep the communication lines open about everything. That means you have to be intentional about interacting with your kids. If you started open communication late with your kids, this will be a little harder because you have allowed them to learn some bad habits. But you can often use a dating relationship to your advantage. You can limit their interaction if they don't communicate with you or follow your guidelines, and you should never be afraid to talk directly to their girlfriend or boyfriend. We have found that the non-family member will often be more open to communication because they want to please their girlfriend/boyfriend's parents. There is nothing wrong with using your child's date to gang up on your child—do whatever it takes to help them grow to be healthy adults.

Setting the Example

Of course, the most important way you teach your children about love, sex, and marriage is by demonstrating healthy interaction with your spouse. Don't be afraid to show your spouse affection in front of your kids. It won't teach them inappropriate behavior; it will teach them that marriage is great. How many kids think their parents are old, boring people who don't have any fun? That is because many parents hide their romance from their kids.

Dad, let your kids see you romance your wife. Let them see you bring her flowers and write her little notes and give her little kisses on the back of her neck as she is going about her daily routine. Mom, don't fuss if Dad shows you attention in front of the kids. Let him kiss you. Do your kids know that you adore each other? If not, how will they learn to adore their spouses? They need to see why you got married and why you like each other. They need to see you defer to each other about decisions and show each other respect and consideration. They are soaking everything in—every word, every action, every *non*-action. You are teaching them about marriage by how you treat your spouse every day.

Defending Your Spouse

Your kids also need to see that your spouse is more important to you than they are. That's right. Your spouse is *more* important. This is the person you have committed to love "forsaking all others." That includes your children. Bill Cosby used to joke that his Dad would say, "I can make another kid that looks just like you." Your kids need to see you defend your spouse to others and to them. They need to experience that you are a team and will fight for your spouse at all costs.

In chapter 3, I mention not disciplining your child in anger. I want to give you one exception to that rule. If your child hits your spouse, the world should come crashing down on him or her immediately! If you defend your spouse more than you would ever defend yourself, your child will learn to respect his parents and will learn a new appreciation for how married people are supposed to watch out for each other. This, in turn, will give your child greater security in life and actually cause him to feel more loved. It is okay for kids to see that they are not the center of your world. It is good for them. After all, you promised your spouse "till death do us part," not your children. And when the kids have moved on to independent life, it is your spouse who will still be there. So let them see a little righteous anger in defense of your spouse. **The greatest gift you can give your children is for them to witness a happy, loving marriage.**

Divorced or Separated Parents

One of the most important things you can teach your child is how to treat the other parent. If you are divorced or separated, it is still up to you to help your child have an appropriate view of the other parent even if your actions are not reciprocated. By watching how you treat your ex-spouse, a child's expectations will be set on how to treat the opposite sex. This is your chance to teach respect and appreciation. It is your job to make sure your children get the other parent a birthday gift, Christmas gift, Mother's Day or Father's Day gift, etc. Teach them to value and respect the other parent and that will pay huge dividends for how they value and respect you and for how they end up treating other people and their own spouse. And don't complain to your kids about your spouse or ex-spouse. Get your own confidant, someone other than your children! Having to bear your marital stresses is too much weight for them.

Don't worry about it if your spouse does not reciprocate your respectful behavior. Kids will eventually recognize who was the respectful parent. You don't need to defend yourself. There is a proverb of Solomon that says, "Like a fluttering sparrow, an undeserved curse does not come to rest." Just do what is right. They may not realize it until they are older, but they will look back and acknowledge that you set the greater example—and they will be better off for it.

How you treat the other parent translates directly into how secure your child feels. Do you want them to grow up secure? Then teach them to value the other parent.

You Have the Power

You have the power to impart to your children healthy views of love, sex, and marriage, and the process is really simple: open your lives up to them and share your love for your spouse and appropriate ways to treat the opposite sex. Develop a culture within your family where no subject is off-limits. Not only will they be well prepared for what is to come, but the open lines of communication will help them through whatever they face.

NEXT STEPS:

- Look for ways to reveal the romance between you and your spouse to your kids.

- Look for opportunities to defend your spouse.

CHAPTER 6

Money & Work

*"A hard worker has plenty of food, but a person
who chases fantasies ends up in poverty."*

A PROVERB OF SOLOMON

As we have discussed, your primary parental job is to
prepare your kids to be healthy, positive members of
society. They need to learn how to live without you
taking care of them. A big part of that, of course, is teaching them
to financially provide for themselves and their families. Providing
for themselves involves what they do for a living, but it also involves
how they handle money in general. Teaching them about work and
money starts early. **You are already teaching them lessons whether
you realize it or not.**

The first thing to do is consider what lessons or truths you would
like your children to learn about work and money and then become
more intentional about teaching those things. For example, if you
want to teach your children that working hard is important, then you
need to give them opportunities to benefit from their own efforts and
opportunities to be disappointed as a result of their own laziness.

Many parents want to give their kids all the things they did not have when they were growing up. However, this often has the negative effect of teaching kids that they don't need to work for anything. When they become adults, they will be frustrated that life in general is not as generous as you were, and they will either end up continuing to live with you or greatly frustrating their spouse or roommates.

The Value of Work

One of the basic attitudes that will benefit your children when they become adults is an understanding of the value of work. Your goal should be to teach them that good things come from working hard. You can begin this early by coming up with ways for your kids to make money. Many families give their children an allowance each week. We did this with our kids when they were young. Each of our kids got the amount of their age. So an 8-year-old got 8 dollars, a 9-year-old got 9 dollars, and so on. The idea was that this allowance was in exchange for the regular work that they did around the house: washing dishes, keeping their room clean, etc.

> **BBH Principle #8**
>
> Children will learn the value of work when they benefit from their own efforts and when they are disappointed as a result of their own laziness.

While providing allowances can help to teach that money comes from work, the downside is that kids can start to think that they should get paid for everything they do. This worker mentality misses another life lesson: that it is important to add value to your family without expecting anything in return. For this reason, as our kids got older, we dispensed with allowances and instead provided opportunities for them to earn money. They were still expected to do their chores, but that was just part of being in the family. Your children should not need a financial reward for cleaning their room. They should do that just because it is the right thing to do (another life lesson), because you asked them to do it, and because they need to learn to take care of what has been provided for them. After all, when they move out, no one is going to pay them to clean their room or make their bed.

For us, doing away with allowances did help to teach our children that everyone in the family is expected to help out, but this approach required a little more effort to teach the work ethic. What we did to handle this was to assign dollar values to extra chores. For example, we paid our kids to mow the grass. The funny thing is, as the kids became teenagers, they would sometimes argue over who *got* to mow the grass because they all wanted the money! This is the kind of work ethic you want to see in your kids.

Now, for this approach to be effective, you have to let your kids be disappointed. If they want to go out on Friday and they don't have the money to do so, you can't give it to them. Otherwise, you are undercutting the value of work. Instead, you can give them a task to perform to earn the money. As long as you are consistent and follow through on letting them be disappointed when they want something they can't afford, kids will learn this lesson really quickly.

Money Management & Saving

In addition to imparting a good work ethic, you probably want to teach your children how to manage money effectively. Don't get discouraged! Even if you are not good at money management yourself, you can teach it to your children. After all, they have very small amounts of money and they don't ever have to choose between paying the mortgage or the electric bill.

When we started our kids with allowances, we told them that 10 percent had to go to charity (tithe), 10 percent had to go to long-term savings, 30 percent had to go to short-term savings and 50 percent was available for them to spend right away. This simple exercise taught our kids a number of important lessons. They learned that you don't get to keep all of your paycheck; they learned the importance of charity; and they learned the importance of saving.

The saving part worked really well. The 10 percent in long-term savings was exactly that: long-term. We explained that long-term meant a car when they were old enough or college or something big like that. Short-term savings could be used for anything they wanted, but could not be used for an immediate purchase. How many times have your kids begged for something in a store but then left it in the car because by the time you got home they had lost interest in it? To use short-term savings, the children had to tell us they wanted to buy something and then wait a minimum amount of time (like three days). If they still wanted it, and they had the money, we would take them to get it. Probably 90 percent of the time, they changed their minds. This not only taught them patience, but they also learned firsthand the value of waiting to purchase something and not acting impulsively.

Lisa and I have never been that great at saving, and yet we have been able to teach all of our children this valuable trait. It is actually a little frustrating how good at money management they are compared to us—but that was what we were trying to accomplish.

The Value of Generosity

Teaching children how to manage money and work hard is important, but it is also important to teach children *why* they work. They should learn that there are three reasons to work:

1. To provide for themselves

2. To provide for their families

3. To provide for others

When our children were teenagers, we realized that we had not done a great job of teaching them the third reason to work. We always told them, "If you want something, work for it." But we didn't make it a clear value that one of the reasons to work was so that you could provide for the needs of those less fortunate. This was a major oversight for us, because we are huge believers in generosity and spend a lot of time and resources toward providing for others. The kids saw that in us, but we had not connected that with a reason to work.

We realized that we needed to be more intentional in teaching them this lesson. So we sat our kids down and explained to them that one of the reasons to work is to provide for others. We came up with the idea of contributing to an organization called *Feed My Starving Children*, where it costs 24 cents to feed a child. We suggested to the kids that each of us feed a child at each meal in addition to feeding ourselves. We designated a jar in the kitchen for this purpose, and each of us was expected to put in a quarter for each meal to feed "our kid." Our children really got into this. Sometimes as dinner approached, they would ask for a quick chore so that they could earn money for their kid's meal. This gave them a reason to work for money besides just to provide for their own needs. It was a great lesson in generosity and was also a fun family activity as the kids sometimes even reminded us to "feed our kids."

However you decide to teach this lesson, your children will be better off if they learn the importance of contributing to society. My Dad always taught us to leave things better than we found them, and that is a good lesson for all of us.

Teaching How to Work

So far we have discussed teaching children why they should work, but you can also impart lessons about how to go about working. It will be up to you to decide what lessons you want to teach, but to help you, here are some lessons we intentionally sought to teach our children:

1. **Do what you enjoy**

   You spend way too many hours of your life at work to do something that you don't enjoy, so we have told the kids to seek out something that interests them. However, we have also made it clear that nobody enjoys their job every day. There are some days that are just plain work!

2. **Do what will provide for your family**

   While we want our kids to have jobs that they enjoy, they also need to know that they still have to provide for themselves and their families even if they can't find the perfect job.

3. **Don't be afraid to explore options**

   One of the great things about living in America is that people can change careers relatively easily. We encouraged our kids to get an education, try the job, and if they don't like it, they can always switch to something else.

4. **Finding a job is work**

One thing we wanted our kids to understand is that finding a job can be difficult. Often landing *any* job, let alone the perfect job, can take a lot of effort. We explained what that effort looks like: applications, resumes, interviews, etc. We talked through how to interview, what questions might be asked, and how to answer them. And we reviewed interviews that they had completed to help them prepare for the next one.

5. **Work your way up**

One of the problems with the current video game culture where you can master anything quickly is that kids often expect to start at the top. And of course many movies with training montages and miraculous boardroom moments for the mailroom kid don't help. We try to set the expectation that our kids are going to have to start out doing the dirty jobs and work their way up. Be the BEST at whatever they are doing now and more opportunities will open up. And we tell stories from our own lives about where we have succeeded or failed at this very thing.

6. **Get the proper education**

We have also stressed to our kids the importance of an education. We are big believers in education and encourage them to study anything that they want. As a side note to the financial discussion, for our oldest child, who we were not quite sure was motivated to begin college, we told him we would pay for one semester at community college, and if his grades were decent, we would pay for a second semester, and so forth. This gave him additional motivation and set a clear expectation.

7. **Understand that attitude is important**

Beyond having the education or skills to do a job, we wanted our children to learn that nothing is as important as attitude. We showed them how in our own company we promote people with good attitudes and don't promote others who do not have a good attitude. We gave them real-life examples so they could learn this valuable life lesson.

Regardless of what principles you decide to teach to your children, you can be intentional about those lessons. Giving your children a good work ethic will help them in both work and school. Teaching them how to manage money properly will give them a lower-stress life. And teaching them generosity will make them all-around better people.

NEXT STEPS:

- Sit down with your spouse and decide how you will teach the kids about money: Allowances? Paid chores? It is up to you.

- What do you wish your parents had taught you about money or finances? Determine the lessons you want to teach your children and start intentionally communicating those to them.

- What do you wish you had known when you started working? Help your kids learn those lessons more quickly by sharing your own successes and failures, but leave room for them to make their own mistakes.

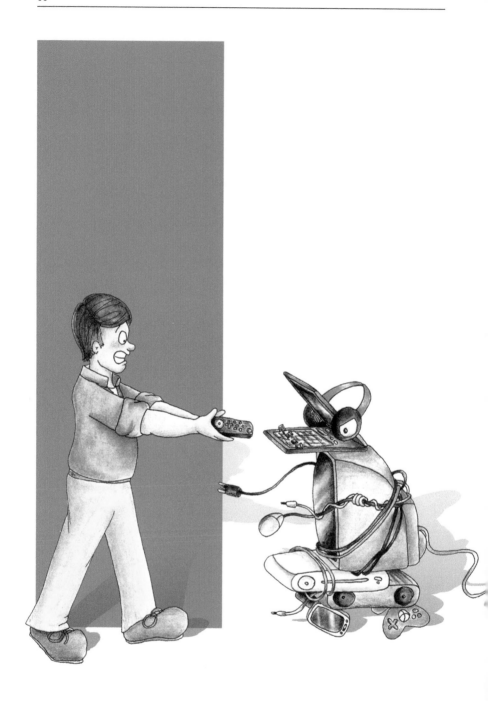

CHAPTER 7

Taming Technology

*"When I surveyed all that my hands had done
and what I had toiled to achieve,
everything was meaningless, a chasing after the wind;
nothing was gained under the sun."*

A WRITING OF SOLOMON

Today's children have access to more technology in their short lives than any previous generation. TVs, movie players, computers, smartphones, iPods, iPads, portable video games, video game consoles, and of course the Internet including Google, Facebook, and YouTube to name a few.

The Benefits of Technology

These technologies have brought our families many good things, including great educational resources and improved ways to keep in touch with each other. For example, in our family, each of our children has a cell phone so we can reach them when needed. We even use the *AT&T FamilyMap* feature so we can see where they are at any time. It gives us peace of mind as parents and it allows our kids to have more freedom, because we know we can reach them and they can reach us if needed.

As a business owner, my mobile technology has allowed me to have more time with my family because I can be reached easily by my clients or employees if an emergency comes up, and I can more easily work from any location and still have the information from my office.

The Internet has provided a wealth of information at our fingertips. It allows us to explore any subject. Often we will be having a discussion as a family and someone will say, "I wonder how fast swallows fly," or something like that, and in a few moments we can look it up on our smartphones and get the answer. As a learning tool, nothing even approaches the Internet. You can find out how to do almost anything on YouTube, from solving math problems to baking a cake to building a balloon that will go into space. Never before have we had the ability to explore *anything* right at our fingertips. And in addition to knowledge, the Internet can keep us in touch with others.

Especially for families with older children, technologies like Facebook can allow you to remain more closely connected, share photos, send quick messages, and keep track of what is happening in each other's lives.

All of these things can bring value to our families when applied correctly, but if we are not careful, these same technologies can add unwanted influences into our children's lives, can build barriers between us, and can build unwanted character traits in our children.

Dangers of Technology

While many technologies can be of great benefit, there are many hazards for families as well. For example, while the Internet opens up a world of knowledge to your kids, it also exposes them to all that depraved minds can think of. Just do an innocent Google image search and you are likely to come up with pornographic images among the responses. Kids no longer have to go looking for pornography; instead they have to actively work to avoid it!

In addition, the very technologies that are designed to connect people can actually hurt family communication. If your child is always texting friends or chatting on Facebook, then they are never fully present with your family. And teenagers in particular can often be more cynical when they are interacting with their friends, a trait that easily moves into the family when kids feel they are in constant contact with their "kind."

The Internet can also undercut your child's sense of honesty as they can download pirated songs and movies—often before they are even commercially released. "Hey, everybody does it!" you might hear them say.

Another danger of so much technological stimulation is that kids are no longer self-entertaining, which results in making them sort of boring people. They grow up feeling the need for constant external stimulation, like rats hitting a bar to get a pellet. As a result, their own creativity is stunted. I am always saddened when I see a family out to dinner where the kids are watching a movie or playing a video game at the table. I understand why parents do this; they are just looking to get some peace so they can enjoy their dinner. And that is fine occasionally. But if this is always the case, they are neglecting their role as parents. See chapter 4 on social skills for more on keeping kids involved at dinner.

Getting kids to sit quietly and stay engaged in a social conversation involves getting them out from behind their screens: smartphones, Gameboys, iPads, etc. Of course, some of us as adults need to learn this lesson as well. One of our family phrases is, "Put your phone away. You're with people now!" As a family, we don't forbid cell phones at the table, but we frown on excessive texting or taking phone calls, etc. unless it is clearly something that can't wait. Of course, limiting the use of cell phones and portable devices during family time is only part of the technology battle.

Facing the Problem

Technology can be a great benefit to your children and can be a great source of danger and stress. Some families respond to this by limiting kids' exposure to technology altogether. Other families don't really believe in censoring their children and so leave the kids to fend for themselves. Neither of these approaches is the best way to prepare your children for a positive adult life. Instead, we should think of technology like we do food. What goes into your children's minds is at least as important as what

BBH Principle #9

Technology is like nutrition. Children need to be taught what is healthy and what is not.

goes into their mouths. When they are young, you select everything they eat and make sure it is a well-balanced meal. As they get older, you give them more input on their diet but try to instruct them along the way so that they know that living on cookies is probably not a good lifestyle choice.

We need to take this same approach with technology. Just as we teach them about nutrition so they can make wise food choices, children need to be taught what is healthy and what is not regarding technology. They need to be able to safely experiment while they live at home so that you can guide their choices and teach them the principles behind them. If you just say "NO" to everything until they move away from home, they are likely to go a little crazy with their choices when they finally have a little freedom. On the other hand, if you don't put any limits on their technology, they will be feeding their minds with unhealthy images and possibly an unhealthy worldview that they may never be able to remove.

Limiting the Internet

Probably the largest area of concern is the Internet. While it is a wonderful learning, communication, exploration, and entertainment tool, it can also put your children at risk. From exposure to pornography and the like to possible relationships with predators, appropriate limits can help your kids through vulnerable years.

One easy thing to do is place all computers in public places so that what your kids are doing on the computer can be seen by anyone who walks by. Depending on the age and maturity of each child, we would suggest keeping most technology out of their bedrooms and out in the open.

You can also use software to limit what sites can be visited on your computer; however, there are always ways around such software and our suggestion would be to use monitoring tools rather than ones that rely on preventing access. In fact, our eldest child reminded us that some children will see such software as a challenge to be defeated, making it even more of a temptation for them. Require your kids to give you passwords to their computers and any online accounts and tell your kids that you can view anything that they do. Web browsers keep a history of all sites visited, and you can go into the history and see where they have been. If they are technologically savvy, they can delete the history, but seeing a big gap in the history should tell you that they are trying to hide something. There is also software designed to track every site visited.

If your kids complain that you are invading their privacy or that you don't trust them, you need to explain that part of your job as a parent is to protect them and help them recognize threats. They don't know everything quite yet, and your goal is to help them recognize dangers so they can protect themselves in the future. Remember that controlling them is not enough. You need to teach them *why* any particular activity is bad for them so that they can apply the principle when you are no longer around. One thing that we constantly try to teach our children is the concept of "garbage in, garbage out." In other words, what they watch on TV and the Internet helps to shape who they are. They should be conscious of what they are feeding themselves electronically.

Time Limits

Even if your kids are not doing anything bad with technology, you should still consider putting limits on screen time. Too much technology can make kids passive. They sit and absorb in a one-way download of information. This can stagnate their own creativity and their physical, emotional, and mental health. For our kids, we did two things: 1) we set a rule of no electronics (TV, DVD, video games, etc.) after 7 p.m. on school nights; and 2) we set the computer user account settings so that our teenager could only use the computer for three hours a day on Saturdays and Sundays. Macs and PCs have parental controls built right into the operating system that allow you to implement such limits with the click of a button. This forced our teenager to read a book or go outside and play or just take a nap—all things that were better for him. And it helped to teach him that limiting computer time is important.

Video Games

Our kids have a lot of experience with video games. They played them a lot while growing up, including all the major console systems and the handheld systems. Our oldest son has made video games his career and recently set a world record by playing one game continuously for over 49 hours. Video games were one way we could connect with our children. We learned the games they were interested in and played with them. I was never as good as the kids but could hold my own as Pikachu in Super Smash Brothers, and I got to know all the characters so we could hold conversations about things the kids cared about. We still have some games we play as a family, such as Rock Band on the Wii.

Having said all that, we think video games have overall been a negative influence on kids, and studies have consistently shown that playing violent video games can desensitize kids to real-world violence[5]. We had a chance to see some of this firsthand when we travelled to Africa with the teenage son of some friends of ours. During the trip, a gunman stopped a line of traffic, including the car in which the teenager was riding. A crowd quickly gathered, and the crowd ended up killing the gunman. Our friend's son did not seem to be moved or surprised by this. He said it looked like what he had seen in movies and video games and that the blood was just darker than he expected. Although it was the only real violence he had ever witnessed, he was already desensitized to it.

Beyond the effects of violence, video games can take away a child's willingness to work hard at becoming great. Kids can master tasks in video games in a matter of minutes or hours. This leads to an impatience that makes it less likely that they will put in the months or years needed to be great at music, chess, sports, etc.

For these reasons, we have sought to put limits on our kids' video game usage. First off, we had to approve the games they played. If you have not looked at video games closely, you may not realize the level of violence, blood, gore, sex, and swearing that have become an integral part of *most* games. However, there is a video game rating system (similar to the movie rating system) that you should be aware of called the ESRB (Entertainment Software Rating Board), and every video game states its rating on its packaging and the reason for the rating (e.g. blood, language, gore, etc.). In addition to this rating system, there are a lot of web sites that can help you review video games and determine which ones are best for your kids[6].

The point is that we should strive for balance. The video game medium is not bad in itself, although there are many ultra-violent and gory games that implant images and concepts into kids' minds that cannot have a positive impact on them.

The real questions are: How are your children doing at interacting with people and family? Are they participating in other things that enrich their lives? How do they do with new people? Problems come when kids lock themselves away for hours at a time, when games become all-consuming, and when they are no longer interested in relating to live people.

We have always encouraged our kids to play multi-player games so there is some kind of human interaction. But we would suggest avoiding online multi-player games unless the other players are real-world friends of your children. Internet gaming tends to be filled with bad language and poor sportsmanship, to put it mildly. If you want to know about this, just ask your kids what "tea-bagging" is.

For our youngest son, we went a step further. We sat down with him when he was about 13 and expressed our concern about video games. We told him why we thought video games were bad for him. We told him we would not ban him from video games, but that we would like him to give them up for six months and see if his life improved (school work, happiness, etc.). He agreed but asked for some concessions in return. He wanted us to set aside a family game night on Sunday nights, and he asked for the right to sit in Dad's chair (a leather chair that no one else was allowed to use). So we agreed to these things, and he went a semester in school without any video games. After the semester, his grades were higher, he was more involved in things like chess, and he was generally happier. He begrudgingly recognized the life improvements, and we jointly decided to keep the video game moratorium in effect during the school year. Over the summer, he could once again play games.

He is now 17 and has gradually reintroduced video games into his life, but they have much less of a hold on him than they did his older brother. He still enjoys playing Gameboy and Minecraft, but he would readily admit that limiting video games is a positive thing.

The Hard Part

If you really want to teach your children that it is important to put limits on technology, then you have to be willing to apply some of those limits to yourself as well. If you tell the kids not to text or call at the table during family dinner, then consider doing the same yourself. It sends a strong message to them if you just let the phone ring and say, "We will check it after dinner."

Even harder than ignoring the phone during dinner is limiting your own screen time. Remember how we had a rule of no electronics after 7 p.m. on a school night? Well, that included the parents as well. We limited our television viewing and Internet surfing in order to make it easier for the kids to do that as well. This can be hard when you have had a long day at the office and just want to veg out in front of the TV, but it sends a strong message of support to your kids, and it is probably better for you anyway.

You can also apply protection limits to yourself with the computer. There is software that allows another "buddy" to see every site you visit on the Internet. What if you asked your teenage son to be your buddy? You would see where he goes, and he would see where you go. Are you ready for that kind of transparency? It would be a great lesson for your son.

Whatever you decide the limits are going to be, remember that you should be teaching your kids the principles behind the limits so that they can apply them when they are out on their own. And nothing will communicate your seriousness about that better than applying the limits to yourself as well.

Kids spend so much time with technology, it can end up being a majority of what is feeding their brains. Help them to learn appropriate technology nutrition so they are prepared to make the best use of it in life.

NEXT STEPS:

- Review all the shows your children watch, the games they play, and the sites that they visit.

- Make sure you have all their passwords and explain to them that you want to teach them appropriate use of technology and save them from the dangers that can be present through technology.

- Again, it is important that you and your spouse agree on any limits you impose.

CHAPTER 8

Kids in Crisis

"Two are better than one, because they have
a good return for their work: If one falls down,
his friend can help him up. But pity the man
who falls and has no one to help him up!"

A PROVERB OF SOLOMON

"Don't lose sight of common sense and discernment.
Hang on to them, for they will refresh your soul.
They are like jewels on a necklace."

A PROVERB OF SOLOMON

E veryday parenting can be difficult. Kids will push you to the limits in search of boundaries; they will often try to separate Mom and Dad to get what they want; and their constant presence can try the patience of even the most conscientious parent. However, beyond the ordinary struggles, sometimes a child can be in a real crisis. And a real crisis can require some different parenting techniques and sometimes even outside help.

It's Not Always a Crisis

The first step is to determine if the issue is really a crisis or if you, as the parent, are just making it into one. In many cases, how you react to a situation can determine if it will simply blow over or will escalate into a full-blown problem.

This starts when your children are young. The next time you see a small child fall down, watch what he does. In most cases, he will immediately look at his mom to see how he should react. If Mom acts upset, then he will start to cry. If Mom says, "you're fine," then chances are that he will just go on about his business. If you are the mother of a small child, try this yourself. Next time your child gets a minor scrape or bruise, don't be quick to sympathize. Instead, reassure him that he is fine. You will quickly notice that a lot fewer things are crises.

Another place you can put this into practice is when working through separation anxiety. Parents who drop their kids at nursery or daycare with a cheerful attitude that this is not a big deal are more likely to have their child quickly give up crying and start to have a good time. Parents who coddle their child at the door expecting a crisis usually get one.

Sometimes you can avoid a crisis by just not treating it as a crisis. As we mentioned earlier, our teenage son decided one day that he wanted pierced ears. We are not big fans of putting recreational holes in your body, but this was not a hill to die on. So Lisa offered to take him to get his ears pierced. Our non-reaction took the fun out of it for him, and so he decided not to go through with it.

Another time, he started talking about getting a tattoo. He liked the idea of a barcode that said "paid in full" to represent his faith in Jesus. Although we have concerns about tattoos, this was not a major crisis. By not freaking out, we were able to talk to him about the permanence of tattoos and how a beautiful tattoo can become misshapen or ugly over time as the person grows and ages. We were also able to discuss how a very obvious tattoo can limit your job prospects. By keeping the communication lines open, we could help him think through the issues. However, if he had announced that he wanted to have "666" tattooed on his forehead or some other offensive image or slogan, then the issue may have become more of a crisis to us.

One way to decide this is by asking yourselves, "Is this really something that is going to hinder our child in life, or are we just worried about what people will think of us?" Remember that parenting is not about you or your reputation. It is about preparing your child to face the world.

Of course, you can't avoid all crises in this way, and sometimes a crisis will spring up on you. When our daughter was young, she would scream when anything bothered her. Her scream was exactly the same when she fell down the stairs as it was when she didn't like how someone looked at her. Obviously, this got old after a while, sort of like the boy who cried, "wolf." We became accustomed to not taking her screams too seriously. However, our non-reaction wasn't always the right response. One day we heard her scream outside and one of the neighbor kids came in to say she was hurt. Our first reaction was, "Yeah, yeah, she always screams like that." However, she got the last laugh (or cry in this case), because when we went outside, we found she had fallen off of her bicycle and broken her arm—it was actually bent the wrong direction. This was a real crisis, one that required dropping everything and spending the night in the hospital.

A crisis like this can be easy to see and is pretty easy to treat: a trip to the hospital, 8 hours of surgery, a few pins in the arm, a couple months of recovery, and all was better—except for the stories and parental guilt. However, not all crises are so easy to recognize or treat.

Dealing with a Real Crisis

Not making the little things into a crisis will give you greater influence with your kids when a real crisis does come along. Sickness, drugs, sex, crime, violence, suicidal tendencies, gender confusion, conflict, unwanted pregnancy—these can all be real crises. If a real crisis does come your way, there are some important principles to remember.

1. **Keep the communication lines open**

    The first principle in dealing with any crisis is to keep the communication lines open. Your goal should be for your child to turn to you if they have a crisis, not go to friends or teachers because they are afraid of you. Don't you want a chance to influence any decisions that they make? If you practice the open communication model that we recommended earlier in the book, then this will come a little more naturally as your kids learn that they can talk to you about anything. (See *Free Time* in chapter 2.) However, you can also prepare for any unexpected crises by talking to your children about them ahead of time. We are hoping that our daughter will have the joy of being pure leading up to her wedding night, and we have told her that would be best. But we also have always wanted her to know that if she makes a different choice, we will not stop loving her and will support her through any crisis that ensues. Don't be afraid to talk about this with your kids. Just tell them straight up that if they get pregnant or get their girlfriend pregnant, you will not be happy with them, but you will be there for them.

If you keep the communication lines open, you have a much better chance of helping them not turn a single crisis into a series of bad choices that really damages their future. To do this, your kids need to see that you don't overreact. We had to learn this lesson along the way. Our older son certainly had things more difficult than our younger kids as we had to learn that getting upset with a kid who has messed up doesn't make the situation any better. Our kids enjoy poking at each other over the unfairness of how easygoing we are with our youngest son compared to our oldest son, but that is often just part of parenting.

Keeping the communication lines open will be a lot easier if you don't overreact. But don't make the mistake of not reacting at all, either. When your child is struggling with something, the issue is important to them, even if you know that in the grand scheme of life it is not that earth-shattering. If you treat their personal crises as unimportant, you are likely to have them close you out of their heart.

I still remember when my girlfriend broke up with me in high school. I was devastated. My mom just laughed and said that it was puppy love, which I would "get over." I don't think I ever shared my feelings about my girlfriend with her again, and she lost an opportunity for communication and closeness. (Incidentally, it didn't turn out to be puppy love, as I have been married to that woman now for over 28 years!)

It can sometimes be a fine line, but it is important that when your kids are in crisis, you communicate your concern without overreacting.

2. **Don't look for blame**

    One of the traps of any crisis is to start thinking about who is to blame. We want to know why our wonderful child is suddenly involved in cutting, or drugs, or crime, or whatever, and we are quick to blame others, our spouse, or ourselves. While there may be room to look for factors that are harming our kids and remove those, playing the blame game is an unnecessary distraction and will keep us from focusing on what is important—our child and their future. You might also find that your child blames you for the crisis. If that happens, tell them that you know you are not a perfect parent, but they are still responsible for their own choices and their own actions.

3. **Act as a team**

    When one member of your family is in crisis, the entire family is affected. One of the big mistakes parents make is trying to "protect" the rest of the family from what is going on by keeping secrets or pretending everything is okay. Your kids are not stupid. They know everything is not okay, and by not involving them, you are missing a huge opportunity to teach them valuable lessons and to draw your whole family closer together. Sit down with your other kids and explain what is going on. Keep the information age-appropriate, but do your best to avoid secrets. This may keep your other kids from suffering the same consequences and will give them a chance to be part of the solution.

There is only one major rule in our family, and that is no lying. When our oldest son repeatedly broke that rule in a major way as a freshman in college, we asked him to move out. We got the whole family involved. We explained what was going on and that for our son's good, there had to be consequences to his actions. Our other children were reminded of the importance of the truth, but also got to see us agonize over how to love our son without supporting his bad behavior. In the process, we all drew closer together.

4. Don't protect them from consequences

As your child's life coach, your job is to prepare them for life in the real world. In the real world there are consequences to their actions. It is better for your children to learn this when they still have the safety net of the family. If your child's crisis was brought about by his own bad choices, then he needs to feel the consequences of those choices. When one of our sons was not doing his homework in high school English class, we did all we could to make him feel the pain of this bad choice. We provided both negative and positive incentives to try to get him to do the necessary work. Near the end of the semester, his English teacher called to say that he was going to fail the class, and because it was a "right to pass" class, he would have to repeat it. We told her, "Good. Fail him," because we wanted him to learn the lesson that not doing the work leads to *more* pain. He would have to take the class again. If he thought it was boring to take it once, wait until he had to take it twice!

There are times when you will have to let your kids feel the consequences of their actions so that they learn the bigger life lessons, and there are times when you will have to create the consequences for their bad behavior. But in all this, you want to always keep the relationship open.

5. **Never withhold love**

Even if your child does have a real problem that you need to address, and even if the child caused that problem themselves, it is important that you overwhelm that child with so much love that there is no question of whether you love them or not. **Don't ever use the loss of your affection as one of the consequences of bad behavior.** For example, don't tell your child you will not hug him because he has made you mad or made a poor choice. He may lose time with you (such as a time-out for a small child, or missing a family activity for an older child, or even being forced to move out for an adult child), but regardless of what happens, your goal should be to communicate that everything you do with him is motivated by love—not anger, frustration, or revenge. If you can bathe your child in love even as you are working through a tough

BBH Principle #10

Don't ever use the loss of your affection as one of the consequences of bad behavior.

situation and letting him feel negative consequences, you will have the best chance of seeing that child come through the crisis stronger and healthier than ever.

6. Determine when to get professionals involved

One of the tough choices in parenting is deciding when to get professionals involved. The easy answer is: seek outside help as soon as you think of it. If you are starting to wonder if your child is having a crisis, then they probably are. Child Clinical Psychologist Dr. Sandra Siegel recommends that parents "trust their gut." She says, "One of the common examples of this in my practice are the parents who are the first to suspect their kid's drug involvement. What they pick up on are little, seemingly minor changes in behavior, emotion, attitude, or schedule combined with the intuitive sense that something's just not right. The parents wrestle with the idea of having a drug screen done, finally decide that they're not being paranoid, non-trusting parents, and Bingo! a positive drug test. And maybe timely treatment that makes all the difference."[7]

Even if your child's crisis is not a major issue like drugs, there are times when an outside perspective can make a big difference. When our oldest son was struggling, we asked him if he would speak to a friend of ours who is a child psychologist. She would not take him as a patient because we were friends, but she agreed to at least talk to him. She spent an hour or two talking to him and then asked him if he minded if she shared her thoughts with us. He agreed, so she explained to us what was going on. Her insights were extremely helpful to us. They revealed to us what his struggles were and helped things to fall into place for us. The understanding we gained allowed us to hone our actions toward him to better show love and to help him out of the rut he was in.

If you feel your child might need professional help, consider asking for a simple assessment. You can ask a professional to have an initial interview with your child to help you determine what any next steps should be. If you are uncomfortable with their approach or if your child does not seem to click with them, don't be afraid to try someone else. In addition, we would encourage you to be involved yourself. Again, a crisis does not affect just one person, it affects the whole family, so at the appropriate time, you might have some whole-family sessions to help everyone better understand what is going on.

You will need to decide when it is best to get outside help. The only certainty is that if your child seems suicidal or intent on personal harm, you should act immediately. We did not face that particular crisis, but we were always afraid of it. We recognize the depth of feelings a young person can feel and how they can be consumed by the crisis of the moment, and so we always wanted to make sure our kids heard hope and love from us even when they had to feel the consequences of their actions.

7. **Don't let the crisis define you or your family**
    One danger of a family crisis is that it can overshadow everything else in the family. Not only can this affect your other kids, but it can damage your marriage. Parents who have kids in crisis are much more likely to divorce. Why? Because the crisis starts to define the relationship. To avoid this pitfall, you need to protect time for your spouse and your other kids. And you need to make sure that the problem child doesn't get all the attention—that is a recipe for creating another problem child!

People can't live in constant crisis. There needs to still be fun and humor in life. Your other kids need to hear that what they are doing is still important, and you need to stay involved in the other kids' lives. This can be difficult. When our youngest child was born with language, behavioral, and learning disabilities, he immediately consumed much of our attention. Because of this, our middle child grew to dislike him. He showed up and usurped her parents and stole her happy home. It wasn't until years later that the two of them became the best of friends.

We inadvertently caused this problem by letting our third child's problems crowd out some of the everyday life of our middle child. Fortunately, we overcame this when they were still young. When a crisis comes on a teenager, the effects on the family can be even greater. If you are not careful, the problem child can end up making the rules for the family, or at least determining the family atmosphere. You need to stay in control and keep in mind what is best for your marriage and for your other children as well. Sometimes that means removing the problem child from the family for a while, or at least from some family activities. It might mean going on vacation without them and leaving them with the grandparents or a family friend who is strong enough to handle the situation. Or it might mean that one parent takes the other kids somewhere fun while the other parent stays with the child in crisis. If you find yourself getting weary, figure out a way to take a break, but don't give up! You *can* get through this as a family. Regardless of the crisis you are facing, you can inject hope into the situation by keeping communication lines open and using your love to give your family a vision of a brighter future.

Dealing with Sexual or Physical Abuse

One special note about dealing with sexual or physical abuse: while the principles above still apply, it is also important that you immediately protect your child from the possibility of further abuse. If you do not, not only are you endangering your child, but you are likely to lose your child to government protective services.

The only sure protection from abuse is to make sure that the abuser never has unmonitored access to your child. This is also a time when you are going to want to get professionals involved to help your child deal with the consequences of the abuse. There are many organizations available to help families that are victims of abuse. Your first step is to get your child out of harm's way and then seek the assistance that is readily available from churches, non-profit organizations, and the government.

The Crisis of Self Image

Our daughter faced puberty early, and by the time she was in middle school, she had the body of a young woman while most of her classmates still looked like little boys. The crisis that overtook her (and us) was brought to a head by a single, insensitive remark from her gym teacher. Her gym teacher used some standard weight scale and told our slightly overweight daughter that she was "obese." This word sunk down deep into an impressionable 12-year-old, and shortly thereafter manifested itself as self-image problems and an eating disorder. It first appeared to be a proper concern for healthy eating, but Lisa was much quicker than I was to recognize the low self-esteem and the food issues. She addressed this immediately and directly. **When there is a true crisis, it needs to be confronted and discussed. For self-image problems, the lie needs to be revealed and the truth needs to be repeatedly spoken into the child's life.** For our daughter, this took several years of both our love and God's love through a girl's Bible study leader to pull her through. By communicating directly to her about the falseness of what her gym teacher had told her and what she was telling herself, we were able to gradually rebuild her self-esteem and restore her proper view of herself.

Even without an insensitive, misinformed remark, most girls are not going to match up to the ultra-skinny, airbrushed (Photoshopped) images of young women that appear all around them. Whether your daughter is overweight or not, she is likely to struggle with image problems. The real lie here is that her worth is tied to her appearance in the first place. As a parent, you cannot usually remove this crisis for your daughter, but you can help. First, you can identify the lies she is feeding herself or that others are feeding her and contradict them. Essentially, the world is giving her constant messages that she isn't good enough. You, as her parents, have to affirm what a wonderful, beautiful person she is and her specific positive qualities. You have to fight the lies. And, second, you can provide boundaries so that she does not make unhealthy choices while she is working through the crisis—things like making sure she is eating properly and not harming herself.

Conflict among Siblings

One thing that has always amazed people who know our family is how well our children get along. However, we already mentioned that our daughter did not particularly like her younger brother for a number of years. So how is it that they were kind to each other? The answer is that we, as their parents, made it clear that kindness was always expected. We did not allow them to be mean to each other. We were intentional in explaining that as they grew older they would be able to count on each other. We told them it was fine if they did not like each other occasionally, but they were always required to love each other. This worked so well, that our youngest son did not realize that his sister had ever disliked him until he read this chapter of our book. And now, they are best of friends.

Your kids will rise to your expectations, and you have a lot more influence over them than you think. But you can also provide them with a picture of the future where they are close friends. They may laugh at that or scorn it, but it will be embedded inside of them, and they will wonder, *is that really true? Will we really be close friends?* And that seed planted can grow into a strong relationship as they mature.

Helping without Hurting

As we mentioned earlier, when our son was in college, he entered his crisis phase. He blew off school and work and was clearly heading down the wrong path. We began by trying to help him as a family. He had a job that required him to be at work by 5:30 a.m., so the entire family started getting up before 5 to make sure he got up, had breakfast, and got out the door to work on time. It was one of those moments where the whole family draws closer together to help one member in crisis. Unfortunately, he wasn't having any of it. After a few weeks, we discovered he was lying to us and was still not going to work even after his family sacrificed to help him. Because he had broken trust with us by lying, we felt that he had to feel the consequences of his actions, so we told him he had to move out. We did all we could to help him. We got him his first apartment and told him that as long as he got at least C's in college, we would pay his tuition, but that he was not welcome to live with us.

This period of trying to guide our wayward son led us to understand why an all-powerful, loving God doesn't just reach in and fix our lives. We longed to help our son. We had the money to bail him out of his self-induced crisis, but we knew that wouldn't be good for him. He had to hit bottom in order to understand the importance of work and keeping his word. At his lowest point, he was actually living in his car. It was torture for us as his family to know that our son was living in his car a few miles from our large, beautiful home. But we had to give him room to grow. We kept a safety net of sorts for him. We paid for his cell phone so that we could reach him and could see where he was via the *AT&T FamilyMap* feature. We paid for his car insurance so he wouldn't do anything that might permanently damage his future, and we gave him small jobs to do so that he could earn cash to eat, but we couldn't help him more until he was ready to be helped.

Throughout this period, we met him regularly for lunch or breakfast and continued to tell him how much we loved him. We made it clear that we were ready to help him when he was ready to be helped. Fortunately, he came out of this crisis a stronger person and better able to be a happy, healthy adult. He is now blissfully married to the girl of his dreams and continues to be one of the most compassionate, loving people we know.

Whether your child's crisis is self-inflicted or brought on by external factors, you can keep communication lines open, make sure the love continues to flow, and provide hope for your kids and your spouse. And hope does not disappoint in any situation!

NEXT STEPS:

- Determine if what you are facing is really a crisis that needs to be addressed.

- Plan a path that is based on what is best for your child and the whole family.

- Don't ever withhold love.

CHAPTER 9

Raising Special Needs Children

"For you created my inmost being;
you knit me together in my mother's womb.
I praise you because I am fearfully and wonderfully made;
your works are wonderful, I know that full well."

A SONG OF KING DAVID

All parenting can be difficult, but parenting special needs children has additional challenges. While each child is different, the parenting techniques and principles we have been discussing in this book will work for almost any child. Special needs children may require modifications to some of the principles and rules, but it is important that you not let your special needs child be in control of the family. **Every child needs discipline and active parenting to help them grow into the healthiest adults they can be.**

We do not claim to be experts at raising special needs children, but we can share some of what we learned from our own experience and from the experiences of our friends.

Our first two children were pretty easy. In fact, our daughter who came along second was not only a compliant child, she was a compliant baby. She would rarely cry. In the morning, she would just stand in her crib and wait patiently until we came to get her. Life was calm and pleasant, and we felt like such wonderful parents. Then our third child was born. He had challenges from the beginning. Unlike most children, he did not want to be cuddled. He would become completely rigid and just scream until he was done screaming. That lasted for the first three years of his life and drove all sanity out of us as his parents. Normal discipline did not seem to make a difference. All we could do during one of his fits was to isolate him and wait for it to pass.

BBH Principle #11

Every child needs discipline and active parenting to help them grow into the healthiest adults they can be.

In addition, he had language issues, which made it difficult to communicate with him. Fortunately, our school district has a wonderful early childhood intervention program that we got him involved in starting at age three, and we credit that program with giving us our child and our sanity back.

Along the way, we learned that we had to adjust our thinking to the way this particular child was wired. For example, he was always asking about his next meal. You would think he grew up in Ethiopia during a famine based on his concern about food. It would really frustrate us that while we were eating breakfast, he would ask about lunch or dinner. At first, we thought this was something to be "parented" out of him. We would remind him to be thankful for the meal he had and to stop worrying about the next one. We would even sometimes tease him about it. However, over time as we came to understand his particular needs, we discovered that it wasn't so much about the food as it was about the plan. He needed to know the plan in advance, and the plan better not change! If we said we were going to the grocery store and then going home, we had to stick to that plan. If we changed our minds and decided to go home without going to the grocery store, he would become upset and say that we had lied to him. It wasn't that he necessarily wanted to go to the grocery store—he just didn't get the concept of a change of plans, and flexible was not in his vocabulary.

Once we realized that he *needed* to know the plan and it wasn't just an immaturity thing, life got better. We would take the time to explain to him what was planned. Of course, changes to the plan were still difficult. If we told him it would take 10 minutes to get to the zoo, and it really took 11, he would again feel that we had lied to him. If his grade school teacher decided that they were going to have recess before math, which was not the normal routine, he could not handle it. You would think any kid would prefer recess, but to him it was all about the plan and the rules. This was a kid who needed to know the rules.

So, what did this mean for parenting? For us, it meant figuring out his particular view of the world and adjusting our parenting to reduce anxiety in his life. We spelled out the plan to him, we went to great lengths not to promise anything we could not deliver, and we gave him time to adjust to any changes that could not be avoided.

We also sought out professional help through our school system. Through that process, we learned that he had a special form of dyslexia. Again, this helped us to adjust how we interacted with him. There is no reason to reinvent the wheel. There are great resources, support groups, and organizations to help you figure out how best to meet your child's particular needs. Remember, the goal is still to help them grow into independent adults as much as they are able.

Sibling Problems

One of the biggest challenges of having a special needs child is all the extra attention they require. The challenge is not just added parenting work and additional strain on your marriage, it is also hard on the other kids. For us, you can see it in our family photos. We have thousands of photos of our first born son … which is sort of natural with the first baby. And we have a lot of pictures of all the children together or of our third son. However, there are almost no photos of our daughter from age four until she was a teenager. Why? Because that is when we were in the thick of it trying to figure out what to do with our special needs child.

Our daughter did not complain. As we've said, she was a compliant child. But she also did not like her younger brother. He was the usurper who took away her parents' attention. It wasn't until high school that the two of them became close. (Now they are very close.) But in the process, we learned a tough lesson. It is very important to continue to parent your other children and give them the individual time and attention that they need even when the special needs child requires so much. That means setting time aside for each of your other children so that they know that they are important too. It means giving them one-on-one time with each parent. It even means giving them two-on-one time with both parents. They need to know they are loved and special too.

Marriage Problems

Another common pitfall of special needs parenting is that the needs of the child can overshadow your marriage relationship. Again, it is very important to carve out time for the two of you. Dad, it means intentionally thinking of how to encourage Mom with notes and flowers and gifts—whatever her love language is[8]. She needs to know that she is still worth pursuing. If Mom is the stay-at-home parent, then Dad needs to be conscious that 24-hour parenting can be very draining, and he needs to encourage Mom to take some time away for herself. It might mean that while your child is really struggling, you have to reduce your commitments at work or church or other outside involvements in order to have more time for your spouse.

For Moms, the danger is that all of your emotional energy goes into helping the special needs child and there is nothing left for your husband. This is one reason why so many special needs parents end up divorced. Dad needs to know that he is still valued as your husband, not just as Dad or as breadwinner or as a coworker in family life. Each of you needs to feel loved and cherished and respected and valued. And that takes time. It often takes time *away* from your special needs child.

Again, there are great support groups of parents dealing with similar issues. You don't need to face this alone. You may also want to seek counseling for your child, for yourself, or for you and your spouse. There are a lot of resources available to help you.

The challenge is to keep the entire family healthy throughout the parenting process and to do some long-term planning if your child will not be able to be launched into life without you.

If you are able to maintain a strong relationship with your spouse and all of your other children, they will be able to help you provide a positive, nurturing environment for everyone. This approach will cause each person to feel special.

NEXT STEPS:

- Commit to carving out time for your spouse and other kids.

- Seek out resources to help you understand your child's special needs.

- Within your child's ability to understand, identify ways to discipline that child and prepare them for the future. Work with your spouse to agree on areas where you can require more from your child.

| Starting a Therapy Fund |

"Do not judge, or you too will be judged.
For in the same way you judge others, you will be judged,
and with the measure you use, it will be measured to you."

FROM THE SERMON ON THE MOUNT

As our children were growing up, we joked that instead of a college fund, we would have a therapy fund for them. The truth is that you are *not* going to be a perfect parent. The only perfect parents are the armchair quarterbacks without kids who say, "I will never let my kids do *that!*" How little they know. Kids are their own people. They have their own personalities, and they make their own choices. Your job is not to force them to fit a certain mold, it is to help them realize their own potential and be positive members of society.

Along the way, you are going to make mistakes. You are going to do or say something negative that stays with them for a long time. You are going to miss some principles. You are going to jump in and save them when you should have let them work it out, and you are going to leave them on their own when you should have helped. You are going to lose your temper from time to time, and you are going to share some bad habits. It's okay. Don't worry about it. Just be real with your kids. You can use all of these things to teach them another principle: **everyone needs to apologize from time to time.** An appropriate apology can have great power:

1. It demonstrates to your children that you value them;

2. It opens up more of a two-way dialogue between you and them;

3. It changes the relationship to be more "real"; and

4. It teaches your children respect and humility.

If your kids learn how to give and receive a good apology, they can withstand a lot of difficult stuff in their lives—and their future spouse will be very grateful to you.

It is important to know your role as a parent because it will influence everything else you do and every choice you make. Every other principle flows from that. Don't be afraid to explain your role

BBH Principle #12
Everyone needs to apologize from time to time.

openly with your kids. Remember they may be parents someday; and you can help prepare them for that day by sharing what you are trying to do, and by explaining when you have done right and when you have done wrong. We overreacted too much with our oldest son when he was growing up, and so now that we are more patient with his younger brother, we make sure to acknowledge to our older son that he didn't have it quite so good.

For example, right after our oldest son, Rob, got his driver's license, he backed out of our driveway into the neighbor's car. He was given much grief about this, and it was a long time before everyone in the family stopped reminding him to be careful as he backed up. When his younger sister got her license, she backed out of our garage right into Rob's car. Who got in trouble for this? He did, of course, for parking so close to the garage. Then when our youngest son got his license, he backed out of the garage into his sister's car. Who got in trouble for that? No one. We just told him he was going to have to face the wrath of his sister for hurting her beloved pickup truck. We recognize the disparity of these responses, of course, so when our youngest had his fender bender, we called Rob to tell him the story as well as our non-reaction. We had to learn to be parents, and as the eldest, he was sort of the guinea pig. We can laugh about it with him now because we are willing to be laughed at. And it is comforting for him to hear us acknowledge that we didn't always do it right.

Be intentional as a parent, but give yourself room to make mistakes and still have a good time. Your kids are resilient, and if you are real with them, they will learn the important lessons along the way.

| Appendix |

The *BBH* Parenting Principles

BBH Parenting Principle #1:
Your primary role as a parent is to prepare your children for life without you.
(Chapter 1)

BBH Parenting Principle #2:
If you want your child to talk to you about the stuff you consider important, you have to listen to what is important to them first.
(Chapter 2)

BBH Parenting Principle #3:
If you love your child, you will discipline him. If you do not discipline your child, you are contributing to his possible failure in life.
(Chapter 3)

BBH Parenting Principle #4:
Don't ever threaten something you are not willing to do, and don't ever promise something you can't guarantee.
(Chapter 3)

BBH Parenting Principle #5:
Social skills help children learn that they are not the center of the universe and that their actions can have a positive or negative impact on others.
(Chapter 4)

BBH Parenting Principle #6:
Use punishment for behavior. Use reward for attitude.
(Chapter 4)

BBH Parenting Principle #7:
As parents, you can have the greatest impact on your child's healthy view of love, sex, and marriage.
(Chapter 5)

BBH Parenting Principle #8:
Children will learn the value of work when they benefit from their own efforts and when they are disappointed as a result of their own laziness.
(Chapter 6)

BBH Parenting Principle #9:
Technology is like nutrition. Children need to be taught what is healthy and what is not.
(Chapter 7)

BBH Parenting Principle #10:
Don't ever use the loss of your affection as one of the consequences of bad behavior.
(Chapter 8)

BBH Parenting Principle #11:
Every child needs discipline and active parenting to help them grow into the healthiest adults they can be.
(Chapter 9)

BBH Parenting Principle #12
Everyone needs to apologize from time to time.
(Epilogue)

| Acknowledgements |

From David & Lisa Davoust:

Many thanks to Lucinda Armas, who has provided encouragement and insight along the way. Thanks to our design team including Amjad Shahzad for a great cover, Anna Piro who rescued the interior, and Sam Sturm for his consistent creativity. And most of all, thanks to our kids for being our first readers and greatest supporters.

From Abi Davoust:

Thanks to my husband Rob for his love and support, to my parents for the encouragement to pursue my art, and to David and Lisa for opportunities and deadlines.

| End Notes |

1 Dr Kevin Leman, *Have a New Kid by Friday* (Grand Rapids: Revell, 2008), 33.

2 "Corporal Punishment Policies Around the World," CNN, November 9, 2011.

3 Irene Ross, "A Consistent Gratitude Practice Makes You Happier and Healthier," *Wellness Today*, Feb. 19, 2013.

4 Thanks to Tim Gunsteens.

5 N. Carnagey, C. Anderson, B. Bushman. "The Effect of Video Game Violence on Physiological Desensitization to Real-Life Violence." *Journal of Experimental Social Psychology*, 43, no. 3 (2007): 489-496. doi:10.1016/j.jesp.2006.05.003

6 Check out parentgamer.net for parent-oriented video game reviews.

7 From a phone interview with Dr. Sandra Siegel, Child Clinical Psychologist, April 2013.

8 Dr. Gary Chapman, *The Five Love Languages* (Moody Publishers, 1992).

| Building Better Humans Seminars |

David and Lisa Davoust provide seminars on parenting and family issues. For more information or to schedule the Davousts for your next event, visit www.buildingbetterhumans.com.

Contacting the Authors

If you have comments, questions or suggestions, please feel free to email us at info@buildingbetterhumans.com.

CPSIA information can be obtained at www.ICGtesting.com
Printed in the USA
LVOW02*1405130514

385601LV00001B/1/P